2 SECOND DECISIONS

2 SECOND DECISIONS

GET IN THE DRIVER'S SEAT OF YOUR
LIFE, WORK AND COURAGE, WITH
EVERYDAY WINNING CHOICES

MICHELLE ROZEN, PHD

To my family

CONTENTS

Part 4: Get In The Driver's Seat Of Your Work And Career

YOU GOT THIS—GET IN THE DRIVER'S SEAT OF YOUR LIFE, WORK AND COURAGE!

PART ONE

2 SECOND DECISIONS TO GET THE SUCCESS YOU WANT AND DESERVE

CHAPTER ONE

2 SECONDS TO CHANGE YOUR LIFE

"Successful people make decisions quickly and firmly. Unsuccessful people make decisions slowly, and they change them often." –Napoleon Hill

You are about to get the most amazing master key to changing your personal and professional life in the most incredible ways. It only takes 2 seconds to change your life. You may ask yourself, "2 seconds? Is that even possible?" It is. It's science. I'll share it with you. You change your life one 2 second decision at a time. In fact, it is the fastest way you can get in the driver's seat of your life, work and courage, no matter where you are in your life right now.

This is the story of the 2 Second Decision—what it is, how it works, and how it has transformed the lives of people all over the world, including my own. You'll find that the formula for making 2 second decisions is easy and simple, but that its impact is extraordinary. It is the formula for changing anything that hurts you, anything that doesn't work for you, any area in your life or career you want to grow and expand. This formula will help you live, work, lead and speak up with courage and confidence. <u>Once you use it, it will become your best kept secret for success in whatever you do.</u>

I created 2 Second Decisions at a time in my life when I was ready to give up. I had a dream to turn my professional life around by going back to school, but everything seemed to work against me. I was a full-time working mom of two very young kids, with no money and no real support system. The economy collapsed, my husband lost his job, and I was just about to give up on my dreams.

2 Second Decisions was born one sleepless night, when I remembered something I had learned in one of my Psychology classes. All of a sudden I knew exactly what I should do, and had the courage and the confidence to push forward. I have since then used it for every decision I make, and it has taken me to unbelievable places in my life and career, beyond what I had ever imagined or hoped for.

I finished school all the way to earning my PhD in Psychology. I have gone from someone who is frustrated with her life and career to one of the most booked speakers in the world on leading changes, a guest expert on ABC, NBC, CNN and FOX News. I have just celebrated 25 years of marriage, and I am beyond proud of my three kids (and two dogs). I feel happy, free and in the driver's seat of the decisions that determine my life. I turned my life around.

2 Second Decisions will turn your life around too. Over the COVID-19 pandemic I have spoken to so many people virtually, and in every Q&A session I have heard over and over again from audience members about how overwhelmed, burned out and lost they feel. Knowing the incredible power of 2 Second Decisions, I have been able to not only use it myself but also help others. Once again I have witnessed first-hand how focused, determined and resilient people become when they use it, as did I. That's why I have decided write this book and to share it with you. I know that it will transform the way you act in the driver's seat of your work, life and confidence, and I cannot wait for you to start.

In the next few chapters, you'll learn the story behind 2 Second Decisions, what it is, how it works, and the science behind it. You'll discover how 2 Second Decisions can change your life. You will learn how 2 Second Decisions get you in the driver's seat of your life, and why this is incredibly important for your success and happiness. Finally, you will learn to end fear, worry and the compulsion for being a pleaser, and to push forward to the life you want and deserve.

You will learn how you can use 2 Second Decisions to become happier, more productive, and more in control of your life and decisions. You'll also learn how to use it to beat fear and take action with confidence.

When you learn the formula of 2 Second Decisions, you're likely to start using it to **push yourself to get the most out of your day.** You may use it in order to prioritize and manage your time, so that you don't run around wasting most of your time on small things that don't really push you forward to the life you want and deserve.

Or you may use 2 Second Decisions to gain more impact as a leader. This when you will use 2 Second Decisions to make sure that you speak up, that your voice is heard, and that you are empowering and uplifting others around you.

You may also use 2 Second Decisions to **beat fear and take action**. You will learn how to put an end to overthinking and hesitation, and know what to do and then go for it with confidence and courage.

While 2 Second Decisions is indeed quick, it is not impulsive. In fact, it is the opposite. You can use 2 Second Decisions to **control your emotions and stop yourself from reacting impulsively.** This will help you with everything from avoiding rash decisions made out of anger, to avoiding impulse buying, impulse eating or impulse reactions toward the people in your life that you need the most for your success.

Once you start using 2 Second Decisions to get out of your own head and take action, you'll be amazed at how easy it is to make 2 Second Decisions that change so much in your life, your work and your courage.

As I began using 2 Second Decisions more and more with leaders around the globe, I realized that making 2 Second Decisions is the most powerful tool a leader can have, and was proud to see Fortune 500 leaders becoming quicker, more on point, more focused and more intentional in their decision making processes, along with the powerful ROI of winning decisions in every aspect of the companies they lead.

As I started using 2 Second Decisions more and more in my life, I realized that I am facing so many decisions all day long that either hold me back or threaten to push me in the wrong direction. As an entrepreneur and a working parent, I found that the number of very important decisions I make every day is overwhelming. There are big decisions I have to make, like in marketing, business and sales; there are decisions I have to make financially; there are seemingly small everyday decisions on what to eat, what to spend my time on, whether to work out, what to spend money on; there are parental decisions on what to hone down on and when to let go.

I found that my instinct was to repeat the choices that I was already used to making—pick the same type of people to work with, yell at my kids for the same things, skip the workouts again (because who has the time), waste my time on small things again, and pick fights with my husband over the same things. When I looked at my life, I realized that I was stuck in cycles of doing the same things over and over again in different ways. I kept blaming my husband, my boss, my family, my co-workers, and everyone around me for feeling stuck in my life and work. It took me a long time to realize it wasn't any of them at all. **I was the problem, because I kept making the same choices over and over again. With 2 Second Decisions, I could make different choices, and get in the driver's seat of my life.**

2 Second Decisions is a science-based formula for making good decisions quickly, by allowing the brain to compute a lot of information fast and reach a bottom-line clear decision. It was adopted from a field in therapy called Solution Focused Brief Therapy, also known as scaling questions. Originally it was used for treating depression and anxiety. I have adapted it to the field of decision making after I heard the kids chanting 'are you 1 are you 2' at my daughter's birthday party, while going through a personal and financial crisis that made me debate if I should stay in school for my PhD or quit. Since then I have used it for everyday decisions as well as big decisions, not only in my own life but with Fortune 500 leaders around the world I have worked with. I have found it to be an incredibly powerful tool for every aspect of life, home, work, relationships, finances and more. I wrote this book in order to share it with you as well.

In a recent interview with LinkedIn CEO Jeff Weiner, Oprah Winfrey confessed, "For 10 years straight [and] every single day, I shook hands with 700 people and I signed 700 autographs."

At that point, a decade into doing her show, Winfrey said she realized there was one crucial question she was neglecting, a question that had the power to change her career and can change yours as well: "What do I really want?"

Winfrey described a day when she had a doctor's appointment which made her short on time, and did not allow her to do her meet-and-greet with guests in between the usual two tapings of her show.

To her surprise, skipping the autographs gave her a boost of energy she did not expect.

"I realized, 'Wow, that's a lot of energy I'm giving out in between shows,'" Winfrey recalled.

"All those years, for 10 years, I had done the autographs because I thought that's what you had to do, because that's what people wanted," she said. "But I never asked, 'What do I want?' I had never said, 'But what do I really want?' I hated it."

Winfrey said that signing all of those autographs felt "vapid" and "meaningless," even thinking to herself about her guests, "By the time you get home you won't even have that piece of paper."

That's when she realized the answer to her life-changing question: "What I really want is to connect."

"What I've found over the years in the multi-thousands of interviews I've done [is] that most people cannot answer that question," she said.

From that point on, Winfrey worked on getting to know her audience by speaking with them every day after her show instead of signing autographs.

"Most people don't know this, but my favorite time of the show was usually after the show," Winfrey said, describing the 30 to 60 minutes she would spend with the audience.

Winfrey said that around 1992, audience members, especially women, would stand up and say, "I did the thing I was supposed to do, I went to school, I got the degree, I even got my master's degree, I did the work and now what? I feel like there should be something more."

If you find yourself searching for happiness and success, Winfrey suggested that you ask yourself the same question she would repeatedly share with her audience—"What do I really want?"

Though time and time again the audience members would say they just wanted to be happy, Weiner added that the more specific you are when you answer that question for yourself, the more likely it is to happen.

"If you know what you really want, what you really love, what really resonates and you have the ability to do that or at least you are in a position where you can learn the skills over time, you can make it happen," Weiner said.

Winfrey said that by reminding others to reflect on their lives, she was putting out a message for people to take better care of themselves.

And so I roll this question back to you. What do YOU really want? What matters the most to you?

How Can 2 Second Decisions Change Your Life, Work and Courage in So Many Ways?

You are 2 seconds away from turning everything that hurts you, and everything that doesn't work for you, in the direction of what you want the most

In this book, I am going to share everything I've learned about change and the power of everyday decisions. You are going to love what this will do to your life and confidence. The best part is when you start using 2 Second Decisions and make them a part of who you are and how you do things. You will not only realize how many decisions you have taken in your life that held you back, but you'll also be amazed at how much more inner power you have than you ever thought you had in you.

I can't wait to hear about what happens next for you once you start using 2 Second Decisions. But I must be a bit too excited because I am getting ahead of myself. Let me take you back to the day that turned my life around: October 11, 2008.

SOMETIMES IT TAKES A PAINFUL CRISIS IN YOUR LIFE TO FIND OUT HOW POWERFUL AND CAPABLE YOU TRULY ARE

CHAPTER TWO

HOW I DISCOVERED 2 SECOND DECISIONS

*"You are always one decision away from a
totally different life."* –Mark Batterson

It all started on a rainy, windy day, on October 11, 2008. I was 37 years old and felt that my life sucked. Back then, I'd meet my good friend at Starbucks at 7 am every Saturday before our kids woke up. One day, I told her how much I hated my job and routine. She looked at me and said, "Then change it. Go to school and change your path."

"I wish I could," I told her while holding back tears. "My kids are so young, and they need me. Adam is in a startup and never home. One day, when the time is right, I'll do exactly that."

She gave me a sharp look and then told me something that changed my life. "Michelle," she said, "you just don't get it, do you? Your kids will always need you and Adam will always be in a startup. Go and sign up for classes this week, and tell me next Saturday that you've done it."

I looked at her puzzled. That never crossed my mind. I never thought of it that way.

SO, I REGISTERED. I COMMITTED TO CHANGE.

Not many people start their master's with a five-year-old toddler, one-year-old infant, full-time job, and spouse who constantly travels. The new 3 am to 6 am shift for studying was brutal, but my life was suddenly full. I was being challenged. I was finding fulfillment. I was going somewhere.

Then in 2008, the economy nosedived. My husband's startup shut down. Feeling challenged moved closer to feeling broken. I told my husband that I thought the most sensible thing for me to do was to take a break.

"I'll go back to school later," I told him. "When things get better and the time is right."

He looked at me and said two things that I'll thank him for every day for the rest of my life. First, "Who deserves a PhD more than you?" Then, "Michelle, if you leave now, you won't go back. Stay with the program no matter what and finish your degree." So, I stayed.

A few semesters in, I found myself struggling with bills, kids, work and school. The juggle impacted my coursework, and I even received a letter from the university saying I was on probation unless I repeated a class.

That night, I cried myself to sleep. I was tired and worn out and felt I had no wins under my belt. Everything seemed to work against me. Perhaps I was wrong about my decision to go back to school. And a PhD? For a full-time working mom of three little ones? With a husband who is never home? What was I thinking?

The next day was my daughter's 10th birthday party. I had it all planned beautifully, with the kids and the balloons and the beautiful cake and all the fun activities. I was smiling on the outside but my heart was heavy. What was I to do? Stay at school or leave? I had a big paper that had to be submitted within a week. I was chanting to myself: should I stay or should I go?

And then the cake came and I hear the kids chanting:

Are you 1
Are you 2
Are you 3
Are you 4

And all of a sudden, out of nowhere, I remembered a tool I had learned in one of my classes called "scaling questions." It was a part of Solution Focused Brief Therapy for depression, and the goal of the tool was to help people pinpoint how they feel on a standardized scale.

Are you 5
Are you 6

I thought to myself: What if I use this to decide, right now, right here, what on earth I am going to do? What if I use this tool to figure my decision out?

Are you 7
Are you 8
Are you 9

My head was chanting: Do I stay or do I go?

The kids were chanting:

Are you 10

And then they yelled:

STOP!

And then it hit me.

How much did I want to finish school? It was a 10 for me. How much did I really want to leave? 0. I just kind of think it's something people expect me to do but it's not what I really want!

I got up. I gave Abby the biggest birthday hug and felt so relieved. So happy.

Gosh, I thought. Now I have to write this paper.

WHO CARES?

I know what I want.

I know my 10.

I know what matters the most to me.

Fighting tooth and nail, I finally got my PhD. The day I received it was one of the happiest days of my life. Not that I liked the ceremony, I hate ceremonies (also, full disclosure, I didn't really eat that morning and forgot my banana in the car, so I spent the entire ceremony thinking of that banana waiting for me after I was done). But what I really felt good about that day was that I had stuck with what mattered to me the most. This wasn't about pleasing anyone. This wasn't about doing what other people expected of me. This was about following my "10" through and through. And it felt whole, and it felt right.

That decision I made at that birthday party changed my life, not only because of the decision itself, but also because it gave me a tool to work with when it comes to making future decisions. The more I used it, the more successful, focused and high-achieving I became.

> In nature, everything that doesn't grow crumbles and dies.
>
> Decide to grow.

I used it for prioritizing and time management, and found myself a lot more confident and in control of my time, both for work and rest.

I used it for making business decisions for myself.

I used it for managing my day-to-day tasks.

I used it extensively with leaders throughout the globe I was working with. I found that leaders used it in team meetings for team decisions, and for their own decisions that they had to make:

- Who to hire
- Who to fire
- How to price
- Outsource or in-house

Instead of being in doubt, feeling indecisive, or taking the wrong turn in life, business or family, I started getting out of my own head and coming up with a number for every decision in my life. I was amazed at the impact it had on leaders I have worked with. I was amazed at the power it had over my own life. I learned to be bold. I learned to be decisive. I learned to take action. And I witnessed how successful and powerful it made others. Change was no longer just in sight. Change was happening right now.

I believe in the power of the human mind to do amazing things when we are given the tools and freedom to make the decisions that shape our lives. I believe in getting in the driver's seat of our life, work and future. I wrote this book in order to share all of that with you.

STOP REGRETTING THE PAST, COMPLAINING IN THE PRESENT AND BEING FEARFUL OF THE FUTURE.

START LEARNING FROM YOUR PAST, MAKING GOOD DECISIONS IN PRESENT AND CELEBRATING YOUR FUTURE.

CHAPTER THREE

THE SCIENCE BEHIND 2 SECOND DECISIONS—AND HOW THEY WORK

"Life is a matter of choices. And every choice you make makes you." –John C. Maxwell

When I used 2 Second Decisions for the first time at my daughter's birthday party, I didn't fully grasp the tremendous impact it would have on my life. I had been struggling for months to figure out if I was making the right choice to stay in school while struggling with a full-time job, very young kids, and very little money to work with. As the economy collapsed in 2008, my husband lost his startup and things got tighter and tighter. When you are trying to make what we call 'the right choice,' you often find yourself wondering **what you are expected to do.** Making a 2 Second Decision by getting out of my own head and coming up with a bottom-line, straight-up 0 to 10 number for what **I knew deep in my heart was the right choice for me,** made making my decision simple.

Fascinated by the clear decision I was able to make, I have continued researching the subject of quick and effective decision making. And whatever I research, I keep applying and using in my own life—with my kids, in my finances, in my career, with top executives I have worked with. 2 Second Decisions became **my most powerful secret weapon for everything.**

When you are not sure what to do, what are you most likely to do?

That's right. Google it.

So how come googling information does not make our decisions any easier?

The answer is simple.

Because there is too much choice and too much information.

Studies show that having too much choice (which is literally what modern life is all about) leads to anxiety and indecision.

The reason for that is that unlimited access to information leads to a fear of making the wrong decision. There is simply too much for the brain to process and it is not able to make a decision, meanwhile not making progress on the things most important for our future and success.

And so we delay our decision, hesitate and deliberate.

It is called Analysis Paralysis.

> Analysis paralysis describes a process in which overanalyzing and overthinking of a situation causes the decision-making to become paralyzed, so that no decision is being made. This can slow your life and your success.

Delaying action while overanalyzing too much information really stands in the way of getting things done. And it is actually worse than that. Neuroscience studies show that struggling to make decisions mentally tires the brain. It is simply costly to the brain in terms of energy. This causes **decision fatigue**. What this means is that when we deliberate and hesitate over a decision, we deplete our limited supply of energy much more quickly, and it is causing us to feel exhausted and overwhelmed.

Throughout your day you make all kinds of decisions, and they are definitely not equal. Deciding which shampoo to buy is not the same as making a strategic decision for your team at work. Because your ability to make high-quality good decisions deteriorates with each choice you are making throughout your day, the most successful people in the world limit the number of decisions they need to make. They handle their most important decisions first thing in the morning, and as much as possible try to automate the decisions that are not important. Former President Barack Obama wears the same suit every day to save mental energy for more important decisions. Most of the time, Mark Zuckerberg wears a gray t-shirt and jeans. When once asked why he does that, he said, "I really want to clear my life to make it so that I have to make as few decisions as possible without anything except how to best serve this community."

Steve Jobs famously wore the same black turtleneck, blue jeans and New Balance sneakers. Albert Einstein had a few variations of the same gray suit.

The science of brain fatigue here is simple. If you are constantly spending energy every day on little decisions that don't matter much, such as whether you should go to the gym that day or have a salad for lunch, you'll become more mentally exhausted as the day progresses. The more you automate your decision-making process, the more mental energy you have to make the decisions that really matter for your future in the most powerful way.

When you make 2 Second Decisions, you **automate the process** by which you make the decision, and you simplify it. Instead of tiring yourself out with long lists and overwhelming amounts of information, you get in the driver's seat and take control of a seemingly overwhelming amount of information—and simplify it so that it is easier for your brain to compute an overwhelming amount of information fast.

Parkinson's Law says that work always expands to fill the amount of time you have allocated to it. If you give yourself an hour to do something, it will take you an hour. If you give yourself half an hour, it will take you half an hour. Setting a time limit forces you to make a decision more efficiently, which will lead to you actually making decisions more efficiently.

Now that you know, based on science and your own experience, that overthinking a decision increases your anxiety and wears you out, let's talk about another problem: making the wrong decision without thinking it through. This is just as bad if not worse. It is called **cognitive biases**.

Cognitive Biases—Brain Fallacies that Kill Good Decision Making

Cognitive biases are mental shortcuts that happen in our brain. They come from ancient history and were actually there originally in order to help us survive as hunter-gatherers. But the thing is this: as much as the world has changed (and keeps changing!), our human brain evolved to its present state over 200,000 years ago, but still operates pretty much in the same way today. So think of it this way. We are creatures with a 200,000-year-old brain, operating in a fast-paced, quickly changing environment, loaded with too much information, too many choices and too much complexity. There is no way that our brain can process all the information around us. It is all just too much. For that reason, the brain has mental shortcuts so that it can conserve energy and make decisions quickly.

Most of the decisions we think we are making with a clear mind are actually controlled by mental shortcuts, ones that cause us to make decisions based on emotional, subconscious biases rather than ones that are actually mindful and thought through.

There are just under 200 different kinds of cognitive biases. Here are the most important ones to be aware of when it comes to decision making.

The Confirmation Bias

What is it?

You are looking for and prioritizing information that confirms your existing beliefs.

Why you do that?

You want to feel more secure about your decisions.

Why it's really bad for you:

If your mind is geared toward validating your existing beliefs, you are not open to new ideas. In other words, you are definitely not open to change.

> You are impacted by the Confirmation Bias when you tell yourself:
>
> "All these people agree with me so I must be right."

The Sum Cost Fallacy

What is it?

You are refusing to abandon something that doesn't work because you've already invested so much in it.

Why you do that?

In decisions that have a lot of uncertainty, we tend from an evolutionary standpoint to focus on potential losses.

Why it's really bad for you:

This is literally throwing good money after bad, even when there is a small chance for success.

> You are impacted by the Sum Cost Fallacy when you tell yourself:
>
> "I've put too much into this to quit now."

The Fundamental Attribution Error

What is it?

You tend to overemphasize personal characteristics and ignore situational factors in judging others' behavior. For example, you tend to believe that others do bad things because they are bad people.

Why you do that?

We know a whole lot about ourselves, but very little about other people. We don't know why they do what they do. For that reason, if something bad happens to us, we attribute it to the events that happen to us, but if something bad happens with someone else, we attribute it to who they are as people.

Why it's really bad for you:

Because of the Fundamental Attribution Error, we tend to believe that other people around us do bad things because they are bad people. For that reason, the Fundamental Attribution Error explains why we judge other people but find excuses for ourselves.

> You are impacted by the Fundamental Attribution Error when you tell yourself:
>
> "You didn't help me because you are selfish and don't care about anyone. I didn't help you because I had a crazy day."

Ostrich Effect

What is it?

You hide from unpleasant facts and try to avoid difficult decisions.

Why you do that?

We love pleasure and prefer to avoid pain and unpleasant experiences.

Why it's really bad for you:

The Ostrich Effect causes you to <u>avoid the unpleasant things that you really must take care of.</u>

> You are impacted by the Ostrich Effect when you tell yourself:
>
> "My dental appointment can wait another six months."

Choice Supportive Bias

What is it?

Also known as Post-Purchase Rationalization, this is when you over-justify your past decisions. In other words: "Since I chose this option, it therefore must automatically be the better option."

Why you do that?

Self-justifying makes you feel better about yourself, and helps you avoid self-criticism which is unpleasant.

Why it's really bad for you:

Choice Supportive Biases close the door on learning. After all, <u>if you do not understand the mistake in the choice that you made, how will you learn how to make better choices going forward?</u>

You are impacted by the Choice Supportive Bias when you tell yourself:

"I know it was out of my budget, but it was on sale."

The Illusory Truth Effect

What is it?

You tend to believe facts that are reported to you over and over (and over) again.

Why you do that?

The reason for this is simple—familiarity. Your brain always prefers what is easier, and it is easier to process information you've come across before.

Why it's really bad for you:

You are mixing familiarity of information with validity of information, and it is causing you to not check facts and information the way you should. When it comes to politics, advertising and marketing, this is a commonly used technique for manipulating your decisions.

You are impacted by the Illusory Truth Effect when you tell yourself:

"I've heard it so many times from so many people, there must be something to it."

The Negativity Effect

What is it?

You tend to be more impacted by negative events compared to neutral or positive events. For example, you may be dwelling on an insult, or keep getting upset by a mistake you made in the past.

Why you do that?

Negative events have more impact on your brain than positive ones.

Why it's really bad for you:

Focusing on the negative causes feelings of helplessness and hopelessness, as well as chronic stress, which depletes the brain chemicals required for happiness and damages the immune system. It stands in the way of good parenting, good relationships at work and at home, and being able to see the good in others and respond to them in a way that would empower and support them. In that sense, the Negativity Effect has a ripple effect.

> You are impacted by the Negativity Effect when you tell yourself:
>
> "Why bother? The world's so terrible anyway."

Here is what I have discovered about making 2 Second Decisions: they don't make life's dilemmas go away, but they do make them get resolved faster and better. That's why it is such a powerful tool.

You see, any decision you make in life defines and shapes your future. Using 2 Second Decisions, you will never experience analysis paralysis, because you will have a process and a tool to help make the right decision for you. You will also not make decisions without thinking them through, thus eliminating cognitive and emotional biases. Every phase of your life and career will require you to make hard decisions. By using 2 Second Decisions, you'll become the person you're meant to become in the next chapter of your life.

How YOU can Start Making 2 Second Decisions in Three Simple Steps

Making 2 Second Decisions is a simple process. Here is how you can start using it right away.

BECOME AWARE

Most of the time you make choices without thinking things through. Your mind is cluttered with options, thoughts and fears. Even when you are not making a decision consciously, you are making one subconsciously. I want you to first become aware of the decision you are facing. Your first step here is clarity.

Because the complexity of your dilemma and the sheer number of options can be overwhelming, I want you to use The VS. Rule in order to be able to clearly define to yourself two possible outcomes.

Why two options?

One option is too limited. There is always more than one option. If you don't see more than one option, you are not looking hard enough, which is why you feel stuck.

If you have multiple options, that can quickly get overwhelming. And that doesn't serve the goal of a quick and effective decision.

When you position two options as one vs. the other, you are not overwhelmed with too many options and you are not limiting yourself to just one.

If you do find yourself in the type of dilemma where you are dealing with multiple options, weigh them two at a time, one vs. the other on a 10-point scale, then the option that scored higher moves on to the next round. This way you will not get overwhelmed, you will not experience analysis paralysis, and you will become decisive and confident with the choices that you are making.

GIVE IT A NUMBER

The brain is forever cluttered. Thoughts, doubts, fears and distractions make it hard to think clearly. You need to get out of your own head. And just give your options a bottom-line number.

When I was debating whether I should stay at school or quit, my mind was a mess:

I was full of fear. Fear that I would not be able to see things through and graduate. Fear that I was not good enough. Fear that I was not being a good mom and wife by focusing on my own dreams. Fear of what others may think of me and my choices.

I was full of doubts. Doubts that I chose the wrong major and career path. Doubts about all the money I was spending on tuition that I couldn't really afford. Doubts that I was good enough. Doubts that I was making the right choice.

My mind was full of distractions. I was a young mom. I didn't sleep well enough. I was constantly behind on never-ending to-do lists. I was overworked, overburdened and overwhelmed.

When I asked myself: How much do I really want this? 0 to 10? My answer to myself was 10. In doing that, I was able to combine both my emotional gut feeling AND my logical brain.

On an emotional level, my gut knew what was right for me. My intuition knew the answer. I just had to listen to my own gut.

On a logical level, I knew that graduating would open new career doors for me. I knew that in the long term, this was my only way out of a job that didn't work for me, and finances that were too tight for the kind of life I wanted for my kids, myself and my family.

This combination of your gut and your logic is critical. In fact, it is the only way to make a decision that is right for you.

In doing that, you are actually using both parts of your brain—your right brain which contains your emotional intelligence, and your left side which contains your logical intelligence. That balance between emotion and logic is the master key for powerful, winning decisions.

Get out of your own head and ask yourself: how right is this for me? To quit school? Take this job? Leave my spouse? Make this investment? Skip the gym? Take this call?

Is it 1?	Is it 6?
Is it 2?	Is it 7?
Is it 3?	Is it 8?
Is it 4?	Is it 9?
Is it 5?	Is it 10?

The number you come up with should speak volumes to you. You assign meaning to it. Anything under 5 is a no-go. Anything above 9 is an automatic green light. Everything in between means you are not sure—you may be tired, worn out, or too overwhelmed to make a decision. In that case, avoid a mindless decision by taking care of yourself first. Go back to making a 2 Second Decision when you are calmer and better rested. You will know then what to do.

TAKE ACTION

Once you give yourself a bottom-line number between 0 and 10 among two options, you will know what to do. In fact, you will know it with such clarity and confidence that you will jump out of your seat. The relief you will feel once you KNOW what your choice is will make you feel in control, powerful and decisive. You will KNOW you are back on the saddle and in the driver's seat of your life, confident and courageous. This will give you the confidence and clarity for the next steps you need to take.

As you use 2 Second Decisions over time, you will experience a deep change in yourself. You will develop more confidence and courage. You will be amazed at how much happiness you will feel by being able to free yourself from hesitation and doubt.

That's what I have gained too. Confidence, courage and freedom. I have evolved and grown so much. My entire thinking process has changed, and so has my life.

Change the way you make decisions and you change your life. I know I have changed mine.

YOU WILL BECOME WHAT YOU CHOOSE TO BECOME, BASED ON WHAT YOU ARE WILLING TO DO TO MAKE IT HAPPEN

CHAPTER FOUR

HOW YOUR LIFE WILL CHANGE FOR THE BEST WHEN YOU USE 2 SECOND DECISIONS

"You are not what has happened to you. You are what you choose to become." –Chuck Norris

When I used 2 Second Decisions for the first time at my daughter's birthday party, I surprised myself at the clarity, decisive spirit and confidence I felt. Once I knew what the right decision was for me, my courage and determination soared. I was willing to do ANYTHING to get to the finish line of the goal I had set for myself, because I knew with incredible confidence what I wanted and how much I wanted it.

Over the ensuing years, I have watched leaders of Fortune 500 companies, alongside everyday people, use 2 Second Decisions for making the decisions that were right for them with clarity and confidence. 2 Second Decisions have allowed leaders to make winning strategic decisions, but also to manage their day-to-day lives better and become more focused and productive. It has also pushed leaders to become more intentional, communicative and empowering in their relationships with others, because it keeps them aware of the right choices in situations that were challenging or confusing. I have seen people using 2 Second Decisions to decide on adoption, relationships, parenting and financial issues. I have witnessed people who thought they were not good at time management beginning to successfully manage their time, and prioritize in a way that completely transformed not only what they were able to accomplish but also their sense of control and calm over their day-to-day lives.

As you use 2 Second Decisions, you'll realize that your ability to get out of your own head and come up with a bottom-line number between 0 and 10, within two seconds, makes a huge difference. You will not experience analysis paralysis because of feeling overwhelmed from too much information. You will not take decisions based on your subconscious mind biases. You will make mindful decisions that combine your logic and your intuition, within just two seconds.

One of the most powerful lessons I have learned both in my own life and with leaders, executives and everyday people I have worked with, is that the most important skill that makes or breaks success is the ability to make winning decisions. Think of it. If the average person makes about 35,000 decisions a day, out of which 226.7 decisions a day are just on food alone, based on researchers from Cornell University. So the better you are at making decisions, the more powerful, focused and successful you become. This impacts EVERYTHING: your health, your parenting, your relationships at home and work, your finances, your fitness…in fact, I cannot think of one area in your life it would not impact. I also cannot think of one aspect of my life and career that was not massively impacted by learning how to make 2 Second Decisions.

If I wasn't sure if I should buy something, I asked myself how necessary it was right that moment, from 0 to 10.

If I contemplated slacking off on my workouts, I asked myself how important it was for me to work out right that moment, from 0 to 10.

If I caught myself being snappy and unfair to one of my kids, I asked myself how fair I was being that moment, from 0 to 10.

If I had to do too many things that day and got totally overwhelmed, I asked myself how important each task was, from 0 to 10.

If it wasn't for 2 Second Decisions, I would buy things I don't need, work out a lot less, get more overwhelmed by tasks, be less patient with everyone around me (somehow I am patient at work but a lot less at home), and make business and financial decisions that were not necessarily the right ones for me.

<u>I want you to fully understand how important it is for you to feel that you are in control of your life.</u> The most successful people, in work and in life, are those who have what we call in psychology an Internal Locus of Control; that is, a belief that their actions have a direct impact on their outcomes. This is contrasted with people who have an External Locus of Control, where they believe it is mainly external factors responsible for the events in their lives.

> The most confident and successful people are those who get in the driver's seat of their life, work and future. Those are the people who accept full responsibility for the choices they make in every aspect of their lives.

Here is why. The belief that your life is the direct result of your actions pushes you to want and achieve more.

People who have an Internal Locus of Control are happier and more successful in life. They know that they are in the driver's seat of their own destiny. They avoid falling into the pits of anxiety and depression.

You have much more of a growth mindset, which means that you are more open to new ideas that promote your growth. One of the reasons why 2 Second Decisions is so empowering is because it turns you into the kind of person who feels they are in the driver's seat of their lives.

Here are the needs that 2 Second Decisions will satisfy in your mind, and why they will make you so much more motivated and determined:

You will feel that there is order in the chaos. You will feel that you have standards and certain ways of doing things.

You will feel that there is consistency in your life. As humans, consistency makes us feel safe and less vulnerable. Knowing you have a consistent system to solve your dilemmas, one that is always there for you when you need it and that you can count on, will make you feel safer and more confident, whatever dilemmas come your way.

You will feel competent. Achievements are the best way to give you a sense of control. There is literally no better way. Even the smallest decision, and the success that follows accomplishing it, will give you a sense of competence, confidence and success.

You will feel safer. You know that there is always uncertainty, but having a consistent system for managing the decisions that create your life will make you feel safer, happier and relieved.

2 Second Decisions ignite powerful decisions. To move, or not. To stay in a relationship and fight for it, or leave. To have your child remain at a school they are struggling in, or change schools. To buy this new home, or that new home. To go back to school, or not. On a business level, 2 Second Decisions lead to powerful moves. To expand or keep the status quo. To hire or fire. To price a product or service this way or that way.

But what actually determines your life is not just the big moves. It is good to have a tool to handle the big dilemmas, for sure. But what defines your life is the smallest day-to-day moves. Because to be successful, you need to be able to guard your three most important resources: your time, your focus and your energy. And for managing these three most precious resources you have, 2 Second Decisions are your absolute best ally.

2 Second Decisions will make you the kind of person who is amazing at managing time.

Time management is the **key to success**. It allows you to take charge of your life, rather than simply reacting to people and events. When you establish yourself as someone who is in control of their time and committed to getting things done, not only other people trust you but you trust yourself. That is the type of confidence that helps eliminate a lot of unnecessary anxiety, because you feel in control.

I want you to not only know how to manage your time like a pro by using 2 Second Decisions, I want you to also focus your mind on the gradually growing sense of confidence and calm it is giving you. Knowing how to manage time, and the confidence that comes with it, feed into each other. The more you know how to manage your time, the more in control and confident you feel. The more confident you feel, the better you will be at managing your time.

You will often hear people say they feel overwhelmed. And you may feel overwhelmed yourself sometimes. (Or lots of times.) But I want you to know this. You do not have to feel this way. The minute you start managing your time is the minute you start managing your life. That is the minute you get yourself out of a state of being overwhelmed and take charge.

Here is what will happen to you when you become the kind of person who is amazing at managing their time:

- You will have less stress
- You will get a lot more done with a lot less effort
- You will become a lot more successful
- You will gain a lot more respect
- You will feel really good about yourself
- You will find that you are becoming more and more of a leader, because you are getting yourself into the habit of taking charge rather than being reactive

2 Second Decisions will make you the kind of person who is focused on what matters to them the most.

Knowing how to focus on what matters the most at any given moment is one of the most critical things for you to learn. I want this to become a part of who you are, to the point that it is effortless to you.

You are thinking about getting to the life you want and deserve, and yet it feels impossible to have that mental focus when you are always exhausted and overwhelmed. How can you focus on what matters to you the most when you are constantly distracted by never-ending meetings, errands, housework, and around-the-clock things to do?

This is the struggle I hear about constantly from countless people from all over the world. So many people want desperately to create better balance in their lives. But there's always more to be done, and staying on top of everything feels like a losing battle.

The solution is NOT to manage your time better or work more efficiently. Or at least, that's not the place to start when you're overwhelmed.

If you are feeling overwhelmed, 2 Second Decisions will give you what you need the most—clarity—figuring out what matters most so you can do fewer things better, knowing with confidence what matters to you the most.

Many people wait for a time in their lives when they are less bombarded with work and chores in order to gain that clarity. This is a mistake, because you will always have more tasks than time, so the moment to figure out what's most important to you is now. As in right now. Today.

I want you to think of yourself as a hawk that can hone in on their goal from a distance. I want you to become that hawk. You see a lot of things, but know how to focus on what matters the most and then hone in on it.

Knowing how to hone in on what matters the most is not just a matter of skill. It is something that should become a part of who you are and how you do things. Once you become a hawk you will never be another bird again. Hawks symbolize honesty and clear vision. I want that clear vision and your honesty to yourself to become a part of who you are.

Knowing what matters the most typically ties into one or two main values in your life. Answer these four questions and you will find out they all lead to one or two things that are very important for you. There is no judgement here—this could be something related to your work, your family, yourself, your education, your health. Everyone is different. But remember this: <u>Life is a lot less complicated that we think it is.</u> <u>And the reason why we feel it is so complicated is that we are not</u>

clear on what matters to us the most. Once we gain that clarity, everything makes a lot more sense.

Question 1:

What is the most important thing in your life? This needs to be something that you cannot imagine losing or not having in your life.

Question 2:

If this was the last day of your life on Earth, what is the one thing you want to be remembered for?

Question 3:

What are you most grateful for and want to have more of?

I want you to use 2 Second Decisions to make sure you are focusing on your 10s. Ask yourself, "What are my 2s and 1s?" They are the clutter of your life, and they are distracting you from what matters the most. Take charge. The 2s and 1s need to be managed better or eliminated.

> "The successful warrior is the average man, with laser-like focus." –Bruce Lee

2 Second Decisions will make you the kind of person who is magnetic to others because of their positive energy

The kind of vibe you give off and the kind of energy you spread plays a big role in the way you feel about yourself, and the way other people respond to you. It is important that you realize that the way you carry yourself communicates to others your vibe and energy, without any words. Without saying anything you can communicate a sense of peace, calm and other positivity that can inspire, uplift and energize the people around you. People get attracted to that kind of energy, like bees to flowers.

On the other hand, you can drive people away from you by giving off negative vibes such as tension, jealousy, negativity and anger. Being around people with negative energy is draining. These are people who make you feel depressed and worn out. After a while, you really want to avoid them. I call these types of people **energy vampires**.

NEVER be an energy vampire. If you are being one without even noticing: stop immediately. And if there is an energy vampire in your life, disconnect or distance yourself. If you want to succeed in your life and work, you should aim to be a positivity magnet, the flower to the bees, the positive energy people are attracted to, not an energy vampire. 2 Second Decisions will help you become a person who is a positive force for yourself and others, because it will help you ground yourself around what matters the most.

Ask yourself: How much is this thought giving me power right now? 0 to 10?

How much is this thought making me weak? 0 to 10?

Ask yourself: How much is this thought really serving me right now? 0 to 10?

Then replace the thought. Understand this: your thoughts are not you. What actually happens is that there are events in your life, and your mind adds its own narrative, its own interpretation to your everyday events, which you accept as truth.

This narrative is often negative, because the human mind tends to focus more on negative things. They are just so much more dramatic and impressionable to the mind. This also goes back to ancient times in human survival. Think about an ancient human mind reacting to something negative going on in their lives, such as a leopard creeping up to eat them! We have come a long way is human, but focus on what is negative and scary, is still deeply rooted in our mind. This human tendency is called The Negativity Bias, and it is the main reason why news channels focus a lot more on negative events than positive ones. People just consume it better and subconsciously want it more, because of the way the human mind works. Only in this case, the news channel is your brain and directly impacts your well-being, relationships and success.

Here is the good news. You can open another news channel in your mind and call it the [Your name]'s Good News Channel. In this channel, you are going to refer to the same events but this time from a completely different perspective, a positive one. This will take some practice, because your mind will crave the negative channel, and the drama your brain wants. With 2 Second Decisions you can quickly refocus yourself:

How much am I on the negative channel in my mind right now? 0 to 10?

How much is it serving me? 0 to 10?

Then switch the channel. You will calm your anxiety, you will feel better, and you will be happier. Much, *much* happier. So much happier and more positive that you will become the kind of person who is magnetic to others because of your positive energy. Your life will never be the same.

IT IS THE DECISIONS YOU MAKE, BIG AND SMALL, THAT SHAPE YOUR LIFE. NOT YOUR CIRCUMSTANCES.

PART 2

GET IN THE DRIVER'S SEAT AND FIND YOUR INNER STRENGTH

CHAPTER FIVE
WHY TAKING CHARGE MATTERS

"There is an expiry date on blaming your parents for steering you in the wrong direction. The moment you are old enough to take the wheel, responsibility lies with you." –J.K Rowling

Before I discovered 2 Second Decisions, if you had asked me why I was upset and disappointed all the time, why I hated my job and my day-to-day life, I would have lots of reasons and explanations, none of which had to do with me.

If you asked me then, I'd tell you that my husband is always busy and doesn't help around the house, that my boss is unfair, that my kids are challenging, that I don't have enough money to do the things I want, and that I don't have enough time to exercise. I would have told you that none of this had anything to do with me. My life was an ongoing saga of challenges, and I was the forever heroic victim of my own life circumstances.

But after using 2 Second Decisions for over a decade, and seeing so many leaders and everyday people around the world take charge of their lives, careers, businesses, relationships, family lives, finances and destinies, I have learned how important it is to get out of the victim mode, and get in the driver's seat of your life. Every day, your life is full of opportunities to either take charge or be passive. Getting in the driver's seat of your future not only unlocks your opportunities, but also gives you confidence and joy.

Using 2 Second Decisions turns you into the type of person who takes charge. Taking charge of your life comes from a place of **self-awareness**.

> Take Charge of Your life, work and future by Taking Charge of Your Self: Enhance your Well-being Through Greater Self-awareness

Let's talk a little more about self-awareness, and why it is the master key to any change in your life, work, relationships, finances—in any aspect of your life, personally or professionally. Think of self-awareness as being able to observe yourself as if you were a third party. In social psychology, we talk about the concept of self-awareness as the type of awareness that allows you to evaluate yourself, your actions and your choices. The way you do this is by comparing them with your values.

Think of it this way. You are constantly bombarded with stimulus and noise. Your days are too busy, and there is always so much to do, so much to take care of, and so much to process.

When was the last time you had a chance to focus on yourself?

I don't mean 'focus on yourself' in terms of taking a walk or calling a friend, though those are very nice to do. I mean in terms of comparing yourself, your behavior and your day-to-day choices with your inner standards. How you think you should behave. The choices you think you should be making.

The process of comparing yourself, your choices and your day-to-day life with your inner standards will likely make you proud some of the choices that you are making, and dissatisfied with others.

> Your road to success begins with the first step you take toward comparing yourself yesterday to yourself today, instead of comparing yourself to others.

It is great to feel proud of some choices you are making. Now that you are proud of them, you will probably keep making these great choices. It is also okay to be dissatisfied with other choices. Now that you are unhappy with them, you are already one step ahead regarding changing what you don't like.

The problem is that, many times, people don't even stop to think and self-evaluate, They have little to no self-awareness. But self-awareness is a major master key in change. Make no mistake. Without self-awareness there is no change.

In case you're saying to yourself, "Oh, but I am self-aware for sure," you may be a bit off on that. In a series of surveys, organizational psychologist Tasha Eurich found that **95% of people think they are self-aware but only 10 to 15% of people actually are.** She cites three reasons for this:

- In order for our brain to conserve energy, we are wired to operate on autopilot most of the time, unaware of how we are behaving and why. As a result of that, we naturally have blind spots in our awareness.
- We are impacted by The Feel Good Effect—we feel happier when we see ourselves in a more positive light. For that reason we prefer to tell ourselves that we are just and right and wonderful, and try to avoid self-criticism because it is unpleasant to us.

- And we are impacted by social media, and <u>social media makes us more self-absorbed and less self-aware</u>. Being self-absorbed means that you are only considering things from your perspective, and that you are looking for validation for your own perspective. Being self-aware means that you are as considerate to others as much as to yourself, and you consider their perspectives as much as you consider your own.

I personally was not that aware of my shortcomings back when I started my academic journey as a psychology student. I knew I wasn't perfect; but to me, if we disagreed, that meant there was something wrong with you. You just didn't get how right I was.

One of the things I have learned in psychology that shook that stance for me was a therapy approach I trained for during my classes, which made so much sense to me that it actually changed my approach to everything in my life. It is called Cognitive Behavioral Therapy, or CBT.

CBT is considered one of the most rapid therapies there is when it comes to getting quick results. I like quick, as the title of this book kind of says about me, so this form of therapy really resonated with me. But here is what resonated with me even more. CBT is based on the idea that <u>our thoughts, not external events like people or situations, are actually the cause of our feelings and behaviors</u>. What this tells us is that we have a lot more control over our lives than we think, and we can change things by changing our thoughts and reactions to events.

Once I realized that I have more control than I think, I felt empowered and got more and more in the driver's seat of the things in my life that bothered me. I stopped feeling helpless in my relationship with my family. I took charge and had heart-to-heart conversations with my husband, my mom, and my siblings. I stopped feeling helpless about my challenging finances and decided to no longer depend on my husband for solutions. I took charge of my career and decided to change my career path.

The impact on my life was remarkable, and I felt relieved, happier and more confident. Along with that, I got more and more curious about accountability and researched it.

<u>What I found was that accountability is the biggest differentiator between success and failure.</u>

The 3 Mindsets of Reaction to Life's Events:

Accountability mode: ownership of your life and your destiny.

Spectator mode: you watch as things fail.

I told you so mode: you put the blame on others.

When you take ownership and hold yourself accountable, when something goes wrong, you go into solution mode. You start to figure out what is wrong and actively try to fix it without blame, guilt or accusing anyone, including yourself. People are successful when they go into solution mode. Teams and leaders are successful when they go into solution mode. Families are successful when they go into solution mode.

This is when people are resourceful and not remorseful. Innovative and not just administrative.

So where is the challenge with accountability? What may cause you not to be accountable?

Accountability goes hand-in-hand with maturity and personal growth. As a young child, you were taught to do as you were told or else get in trouble. As a student, you had to follow the directions you were given or else get poor grades. As an employee, you must do what your boss says or else you may lose your job. As a result of that, you develop a mindset that being accountable to your actions means you need to comply with the demands of others. When were you actually taught to be accountable to yourself?

On a conscious level this is an issue of lack of training. On a subconscious level, lack of accountability is a bad habit that becomes a part of how you do things when your mind is on autopilot. You simply get used to not holding yourself accountable, and blaming the situation, the government, the weather, or the other people around you. Anyone but yourself.

> "Don't find fault. Find a remedy. Anyone can complain." –Henry Ford

The day I started using 2 Second Decisions was the day I started holding myself accountable to my own life and choices. It wasn't about the economy that had collapsed, it wasn't about the professor who didn't like me, it wasn't about anything but me holding myself accountable to my own choices.

<u>Getting in the driver's seat of your life is the right way to lead your own life. This is your right and your obligation to yourself.</u> It's not a matter of education, money, personality or circumstances. It's simply a matter of taking charge and getting out of passive victim mode. It's a matter of dropping all the reasons, explanations and excuses.

But accountability alone is not enough. The speed of holding yourself accountable is just as important.

In his book *Outwitting the Devil*, Napoleon Hill talks about a time in his life when he was completely desperate. His life had hit such rock-bottom that he just didn't care what people thought about him anymore. From that place of desperation, he decided to listen to his inner voice and to what his gut was telling him, and to act immediately. He didn't allow himself to hesitate.

Recent research done at Yale University shows that if you hesitate for even just a few seconds when you feel inspired to do something, your chances of acting drop drastically. The researchers concluded that if you feel inspired to do something, you must act immediately. Every second counts.

> "He who hesitates is lost." –Cato

At a personal and professional rock-bottom, Hill entered a state of infinite power. He acted quickly and confidently on promoting his goals and pushing forward from the lowest point of his life.

Tony Robbins explains this notion of getting in the driver's seat of quick and decisive action as a three-part process:

1. **Make** a decision while you are in a passionate or peak state
2. **Commit** to that decision by removing everything in your environment that conflicts, and by creating multiple accountability mechanisms
3. **Resolve within yourself** that what you have decided is *a done deal.* It will happen.

There are two kinds of people in the world: those who get the results they want for their life, work and future; and those who are great at finding excuses for why they didn't get the results. In the Star Wars saga, when Yoda hears Luke's remark about his uncertainty in getting his ship out of a swamp, he is quick to reprimand him with what has become one of the most famous phrases in film history: "Do or do not. **There is no try.**" He knows that if Luke simply tries then he will fail, because he has already doubted his abilities.

Taking Charge and Getting in the Driver's Seat Matters. Here is What You Should Do About It:

I want to talk to you about getting in the driver's seat of your life, because I know how remarkably my life changed when I got in the driver's seat of mine, and I have since been researching the topics of accountability and commitment for over a decade.

You see, accountability and commitment to get the best results for yourself is not about willpower. They are a reflection of your relationship with yourself. When you are not committed to yourself, and not holding yourself accountable to your own life, then you do not love yourself enough.

Most people have an incredibly weak relationship with commitment and accountability. People break commitments and find excuses all the time. People also lie to themselves all the time. Most people are too afraid to commit to anything, because they already know deep inside that they are going to break the commitment. Most people are too afraid to hold themselves accountable, because they know that holding themselves accountable means work.

Commit. Get in the driver's seat of your life, work and future. Let the rest of the world make excuses. Not you. When you make a commitment, you develop a self-concept that lines up with your new goal. You begin to see yourself based on the new person you are going to become, based on the commitment you have made, and you change your behavior to align with that.

Publicly commit to get in the driver's seat of something in your life TODAY. Ask yourself, on a scale of 0 to 10, how much does it matter to you? How strongly do you feel about it?

Are you 1?
Are you 2?
Are you 3?
Are you 4?
Are you 5?
Are you 6?
Are you 7?
Are you 8?
Are you 9?
Are you 10?

Commit to your 10s TODAY. Get in the driver's seat of your work, life and future. Take charge of your own destiny and steer the wheel of the boat which is your life in the direction you want it to go, no matter how turbulent the water.

WRITE THE SCRIPT OF YOUR OWN LIFE. YOU ARE THE ONLY ONE THAT CAN WRITE IT.

CHAPTER SIX

TAKE CHARGE OF YOUR DAY AND TIME

"Ordinary people think merely of spending time. Great people think of using it." –Arthur Schopenhauer

Managing your time is managing your life.

When I used 2 Second Decisions to make the decision that changed my life—to stay the course, graduate with my PhD, and not drop out no matter how challenging things were—I prioritized more than just my career and education goals. I prioritized myself.

From that point on, I learned to use 2 Second Decisions to prioritize what matters to me the most at any given moment. As a full-time working mom of three very young kids and a full-time student, I had to constantly pick and choose, quickly and efficiently, what matters the most at any given moment. How would I do all of that with just 24 hours in a day, without losing my mind, losing my marriage, losing sight of what was going on with my kids, losing my job, or failing classes? How would I do all of that without losing myself? And how on Earth would I make sure that people in the house actually had clean socks to wear or clean uniforms for soccer?

Losing my mind was not an option. I don't do very well when I lose my mind, and I am also not very nice when that happens.

Losing my marriage was out of the question. I lucked out on a guy who I really love.

Losing sight of what was happening with my kids was also out of the question. I watched all three of them like a hawk. Nothing in the world is as dear to my heart as those three kids.

Losing my job was not an option financially, and I'd already made up my mind that I was not dropping out of school.

Clean socks are kind of important, but for sure no one in my house has worn matching socks for years (matching socks are so overrated).

So my only choice was to get really good at two things: massive time management skills and forgiving myself as often as I could. But before we even start talking about time management, I want to put forgiving yourself right here as #1 on the list of time management strategies.

You see, the biggest enemy of time management is perfectionism. When you are dealing with a lot, failing to forgive yourself will get you completely overwhelmed. There is just no way for things to be perfect. Something has to give, and you are going to have to live with the fact that you drop some balls, that you forget birthday parties, that you mix up days on soccer practices, and that your kids have to remind you four times to fill out that school form.

But you will know who their friends are and you will know what is going on with each friend. You will know what hurts them and scares them and you will be there to wipe their tears and help them figure things out.

You will learn to prioritize your spouse because this relationship is the foundation of your family and everything it is built on. And it will give both of you strength and joy. Your spouse comes before your kids.

Not being there for the people you love is not an option.

Not taking care of yourself is not an option.

You forgive yourself for the things that matter less to you.

What are your 9s and 10s? What are your 2s and 1s and 0s?

Only you decide.

> Time is one of the most precious resources you have.

The more I work with leaders and people around the world on prioritizing and managing time, the more I have found deeply rooted misconceptions about time management that stand in the way of people's success. I want us to take a look at those misconceptions together. Where do you see your own misconceptions in them? Where do you need to change your relationship with time, and your mindset toward managing it?

Myth: You Need to Plan Every Part of Your Day to Be Productive

Spoiler alert, there is always one major factor that ruins the idea of planning every part of your day: real life. I do not believe in rigid time management because I do not believe in anything rigid. Some days you have more energy than others. Some days you've slept better or worse. Some unexpected things might have come up. Your kid is sick. Your heat broke. Your mom needs your help. If you are not ready to deal with the fact that the only constant thing in your life is change, and think that you can lead a rigid time management regiment, you are holding on to a perfectionist, unrealistic plan that you need to let go of. Rigid plans don't work.

> "Overplanning kills magic." –Edan Lepucki

Myth: Multitasking Helps You Get More Done in Less Time

Spoiler alert, you are reading the book of a recovered multitasker. I was literally the worst, doing five things at the same time and feeling really proud of myself. Let's count the damages: I burned lots of pots, I cut my fingers by mistake way too many times, I fell down the stairs, and I sent the wrong email to the wrong teacher. Until I read and researched and found out why all of these things were happening to me, and why I should stop.

I found countless studies that explained why multitasking results in less productivity and more mistakes. Every time I read another article, it felt like they were talking about me. Ask my kids how many burnt dinners were happening in my house at the time. And to think that I actually took pride in my ability to multitask!

I discovered that the prefrontal cortex of the brain starts working every time you need to pay attention. Scientists at the Institut National de la Santé et de la Recherche Médicale in Paris found that when you work on a single task, it means that both sides of the prefrontal cortex are working together in harmony. Adding another task forces the left and right sides of the prefrontal cortex to work independently. This way, your brain splits its energy in half and causes you to forget details and make mistakes.

A study by the University of London showed that multitasking also leads to a temporary decline in your IQ score, similar to someone who has stayed up all night, in some cases by 15 points, and in other cases leaving the person with an IQ equivalent to that of an eight-year-old child.

Here are the two alternatives to multitasking, because working with an IQ equivalent to that of an eight-year-old is really not a very good idea.

One alternative to multitasking is literally doing one thing at a time. Science shows that when you focus on a single task, you feel less stress and actually enjoy the task much more. Productivity in the most basic sense is about getting the most out of your time. Single tasking gets you into deeper focus, and you will be up to 500% more productive compared to multitasking.

Yes, doing one thing at a time can get boring at first, especially if you are ADHD like me. But once you stop multitasking and force yourself to focus on one thing at a time, you will be amazed at your own creativity and productivity.

In his book *Thinking, Fast and Slow*, Nobel Prize-winning psychologist and economist Daniel Kahneman details how our brains have two processing mechanisms: an older, faster "automatic" system; and a newer, rational "controlled" system. Kahneman refers to these as System 1 (automatic) and System 2 (controlled).

In *The Happiness Hypothesis*, New York University psychologist Jonathan Haidt describes the key distinction between "automatic processing" and "controlled processing" as it relates to multitasking: controlled processing is limited—we can think consciously about one thing at a time only—but automatic processes run in parallel and can handle many tasks at once. If the mind performs hundreds of operations each second, all but one of them must be handled automatically.

If you're going to do two things at once, they can't compete for the same cognitive resources, because the controlled system can only handle one thing at a time. In his book *Indistractable*, Nir Eyal names it "multichannel multitasking." It's when you pair a focused task with an automatic task.

For example, you can have a walking work meeting (walking can help you think better—I schedule walk meetings all the time). You can also listen to a podcast while folding laundry. Notice that in the automatic tasks you are using your body, but in the focused tasks you are using your mind.

Time management is about prioritizing at any given moment. It is about laser focusing your most precious resources—time, focus and energy—on what matters the most.

Is this 1?
Is this 2?
Is this 3?
Is this 4?
Is this 5?
Is this 6?
Is this 7?
Is this 8?
Is this 9?
Is this 10?

A day that was spent running around spending time and energy on 2s and 3s, busy and worn out and not even getting to your 9s and 10s, is a wasted day.

> "People who can focus, get things done. People who can prioritize, get the right things done."
> –John Maeda

There is so much talk about creating a to do list or not creating a to do list, and if it is necessary and helpful at all. So let me tell you this. Without a to do list, your day is a mess. There is no way to be productive without a to do list. The problem comes up when you create a long to do list, don't get to many of the things that are on it (41% percent of all to-do list items never actually get done, according to research from the project-tracking software provider iDoneThis).

The problem with generic to-do lists is that they do not set priorities. How silly is it if the 41% of the to-do list you don't get to are your 9s and your 10s, while you've knocked off your 2s, 3s and 4s, and didn't really stop to prioritize?

2 Second Decisions turn any generic to-do list to a priorities-based to-do list, and boosts your productivity to new and exciting levels. <u>It turns you into a person who gets the most important things done. A successful, focused and intentional person who gets what matters the most done.</u>

Here is an example:

10	Call Sue	10	Pay electric bill
6	Call Bob	5	Take out the dry cleaning
10	Call client	10	Handle school forms
8	Call Mom	2	Wash car
10	Email proposal to client	2	Find Christmas presents
7	Email Emily's teacher	4	Organize paperwork

When I started using 2 Second Decisions not just for the big decisions in my life, but also the seemingly smaller decisions of where to spend my time and what to focus on, I drastically improved the way I ran my day-to-day life, and my stress levels dropped significantly. How do we spend so many days at school learning so many things, but not learn how to manage our time and prioritize?

Some days are so crazy and I feel so tired. I am either back from a flight and suffering jetlag, or just had a bad day, or just don't have any patience to even create a to-do list. For those days, I use what I call a 'little list,' a sticky note with just a handful of my 10s that absolutely must happen that day no matter what. It takes me two seconds to put together, and I find that it is very helpful.

I also found that crossing things off my lists makes me feel good. When I taught my youngest daughter, Mia, to work with a to-do list when she was in 5th grade, she made sure to leave space for the checkmark next to each thing on her list, and she loved checking things off. The expression on her face at the end of each day when she proudly showed me her checked-off list was priceless.

I want you to use this mind hack because it will directly and positively impact your performance. When you check things off a list, your brain reads it as success and releases dopamine, which is connected to feelings of pleasure, learning and motivation. When you feel the effects of dopamine, you are excited to repeat the action that made you feel this good. Neuroscientists call this 'self-directed learning.' This means you are training your brain to want to get more done because it feels good. As simple as that.

A common mistake many people make when they create a to-do list is that they overwhelm themselves with writing down projects, instead of tasks. Here is what the difference between the two look like:

Instead of writing "write my next book" (project), write "create table of contents" (task)

Instead of writing "look for possible homes to buy" (project), write "call the realtor" (task)

And of course, we can't talk about time management without talking about procrastination. Here is the science about procrastination that you need to know. **Procrastination is a learned behavior. Family members role-model it to other family members, who then repeat**

it. Studies show that procrastination is a self-defeating behavior and can have lasting effects on our lives, including compromised physical and emotional health.

I want to communicate to you clearly what this means. It means that when you procrastinate, your kids are watching you. They are learning this self-sabotaging behavior from you, and they will procrastinate themselves.

When you procrastinate you are subconsciously sabotaging your success. And you are teaching your kids to do the same. Procrastination is self-sabotage in disguise, and it is indicative of low self-esteem and lack of self-confidence.

So alongside using 2 Second Decisions to prioritize and get the most important things done, I want you to get to the root of the problem: you. You don't believe in yourself, and you are hurting yourself subconsciously.

The best way to handle a self-sabotaging subconscious is to work with a positive affirmation that you keep repeating to yourself. This way, you "brainwash" yourself and make your mind work with you, rather than against you.

I want you to repeat to yourself over and over again throughout your day:

"I take charge and get things done."

Then create a to-do list and number out your priorities 0 to 10. Focus on your 9s and 10s first, and keep repeating to yourself:

"I take charge and get things done."

This positive affirmation, together with 2 Second Decisions, will turn you into exactly that, the kind of person who takes charge and gets things done. By doing so, you are not only growing to become the successful person you want and deserve to be, you are also becoming a role model to others to follow.

IT IS NEVER GOING TO BE
THE RIGHT TIME. TAKE
THE FIRST STEP.

CHAPTER SEVEN

TAKE CHARGE OF YOUR SUCCESS

"The only person you are destined to become, is the person you decide to be." –Ralph Waldo Emerson

You may be wondering what courage has to do with living to your full potential, or in other words living the life you want and deserve. If you ask yourself what the one thing is that's linked to all success, I am willing to bet you would not have said the word 'courage.' But guess what? Understanding what courage has to do with your ability to become who you can be is your master key. There are two opposing forces in your life, and they are pulling you in completely different directions: fear and courage.

Courage is the strength to do something in the face of pain or possible pain.

Fear is the motion caused by the belief that someone or something is dangerous or a threat, and may cause pain.

Courage and fear are the two opposing forces on your journey to living the life you want and deserve.

Are you afraid to be different?
Or do you have the guts to be different?

When you are in the process of making decisions, I suspect you have the impulse to look and see what others are doing. This is a common human phenomenon which has been studied by social scientists for a long time. What social science researchers have found is that people tend to look to the opinions of others, especially when they are unsure of themselves and the situation is uncertain. Research on conformity clearly shows consistently that people tend to follow others even when they clearly see that what those other people are doing is wrong.

Why are we so compelled to follow the crowd, even when we know that the choice is wrong, and why are we so influenced by peer pressure? To keep up with the Joneses? To follow the crowd?

Like everything else you do when you work toward your success, you are once again working against your own brain. This is more than doable, but requires awareness and focus. You see, research shows that social influences actually change your perceptions and memories. So, rather than knowingly making the wrong choice just to conform to peer pressure, the influence of others actually changes what you see as the correct choice. Beyond that, people (including you) have 'herding brains' with built-in components that monitor how aligned we are with others, and make us feel good when we follow the crowd just like everyone else.

The neurochemical oxytocin triggers a 'bliss response' in your brain whenever you are engaging in social behavior. This is because your brain is an incredible survival machine. One of your most effective subconscious mechanisms is belonging to a group, which is why the bliss response makes you feel warm, safe and happy. If you lack that feeling, your brain will trigger you to seek the connections that will make you feel that way.

It is easy to say "fight the herd instinct in yourself," but there is a much easier way to do it: use 2 Second Decisions to check your social environment. Ask yourself this: on a scale of 0 to 10, how much is your social circle good for pushing you toward achieving your goals?

In *The Master Mind Principle*, Napoleon Hill says, "Deliberately seek the company of people who influence you to think and act on building the life you desire. Two or more people actively engaged in the pursuit of a definite purpose with a positive mental attitude, constitute an unbeatable force."

> "The first step toward success is taken when you refuse to be a captive of the environment in which you find yourself." –Mark Caine

It seems easiest to be like everyone else. Your courage is about the decision to be different. To do something different. And to support yourself by choosing people who can stomach that, support you and support your courage. You may find that you outgrow old relationships, and that you have little to no tolerance to people who can't handle the fact that you are making new and exciting decisions that push you to new and exciting places. That's okay. Stick with the people who support the brave, decisive and courageous person that you are becoming.

Are you afraid of doing the work?
Or do you have the courage to do the work?

You see others succeed. You see them win awards and prizes, overcome tremendous challenges, make more money, get promoted, and build successful businesses. You think they are in another league, living another kind of life in another dimension where this kind of success is possible. Or you might have people in your circle of friends who live their dreams, get their ideal job, and do what they've always wanted to do. You might think, *Why them? Why did they succeed? Why not me? Why are they so lucky? What do they have that I don't?*

When we talk about courage to do the work, it's not about having courage to work hard. A lot of people work hard, and they still don't get the life they want and deserve. What I am talking about is much more difficult—working on yourself.

It is easier to work at your job than to work on yourself. It is easier to work at the gym than to work on yourself. Anything is easier than to work on yourself, because working on yourself means working on changing the way you see and do things, and that can be quite scary.

Your success is the direct result of your work on yourself, your skills and your mindset, using every opportunity you have to become better tomorrow than you were yesterday. Your life is not a matter of being. It is a journey of becoming. And becoming takes courage because it requires you to live way out of your comfort zone.

You know what the hardest part of having the courage to do the work was for me? It was letting go of the idea that I am wonderful. I am always in a position of learning how to be better, which means that I am always far away from my comfort zone. I don't even remember what my comfort zone looks like anymore. I have accepted the challenge to always face my mistakes and never hide from them. I have accepted to face my shortcomings and try to do better. I have accepted to always climb the metaphorical mountain of a new challenge. Even though it makes my knees metaphorically hurt (though in real life they are not that great either), I have gotten into the habit of always facing challenges knowing full-well that it will involve work, learning new skills, and pushing myself to become better.

I didn't used to be that way, but now I know no other way. What changed was the first time I understood the magnitude of the reward for living outside your comfort zone. Things picked up in my life and career and went to places I never thought possible. Once you taste the reward of living out of your comfort zone, you are never going back again.

I actually now dread the comfort zone. I don't want to be numb. I prefer the climbing and the pain in the knees.

Are you hiding behind your dreams of success? Or do you have the guts to act now?

Many people dream of success and they will gladly share their dreams with you. But they never have the courage to act. They never have the guts to go ahead with it.

You may be thinking that people who dream of success but don't take action are afraid of failure, and that may be the case. But there is another fear a lot more debilitating that you may not be thinking about, and that is the fear of success. It may sound counter-intuitive, but many people are actually scared of achieving what they really want. This fear may be subtle, and it may be harder to recognize, but it is a lot more real than you think.

"You must do the thing you think you cannot do."
–Eleanor Roosevelt

Success means change—does it scare you?
Even if it's the change you've always wanted?

If you try something and fail, you go back to what you knew. You may not be happy about it, but you go back to your comfort zone.

If you try something and succeed, you head into new territory. Things are different. Things change. And that may be scary.

If you ask yourself, *What if I fail?*, you will find that the answer is easy and almost reassuring. You just go back to what you know and have (or not have) now.

Here is the bigger question for you to face. Ask yourself, *What if I actually pull this off?*

Everything would be different, and you wouldn't even really know all the ways things would be different right away. It would be completely new territory.

I can't take fear away from you. That fear is there and it is going nowhere.

I can tell you what I did. I looked at it dead in the eye and I asked myself, *How much do I want this? 0 to 10? How much do I want to change my life?*

My answer was 10. And here is where the magic lies. Where the 10s are, fear still exists. You just care about it a lot less.

Do you back off when you fail?
Or do you have the guts to move on?

Have you ever been so afraid of failing at something that you decided not to try it at all? Has a fear of failure meant that, subconsciously, you undermined your own efforts to avoid the possibility of a larger failure?

If we are going to talk about what you do when you fail, back off or move on, we have to talk about not failure itself, but the fear of it.

Many of us are afraid of failing, at least some of the time. But fear of failure (technically known as "atychiphobia") is when you allow that fear to stop you from doing the things that can move you forward to achieve your goals.

Fear of failure can be linked to many causes. For instance, having critical or unsupportive parents can be a factor for some people. Because they were routinely undermined or humiliated in childhood when something didn't go right, they associate failure with humiliation and loss of love and support.

Experiencing a traumatic event at some point in your life can also be a cause. If you have had a traumatic failure, you carry that fear of failure even now, years later.

I want you to check out these symptoms of fear of failure. Do you see yourself in any of these?

- Are you reluctant to try new things?
- Are you reluctant to get involved in challenging projects?
- Do you self-sabotage? Work against your own interests without even understanding why?
- Do you procrastinate?

- Do you have excessive anxiety, to the point that you can't follow through with goals?
- Do you have low self-confidence, and tend to say negative things about yourself and your ability to succeed?
- Are you a perfectionist, and tend to avoid doing anything you know you cannot do perfectly and totally successfully?

It's almost impossible to go through life without experiencing some kind of failure. The few people who manage to do so live so cautiously that they go nowhere. People who do this are not really living at all.

It takes courage to live the life you want and deserve!

It takes courage to change your life. It takes courage to move from what you know, even if you don't like it or want it, to something unknown and uncertain.

Everything in life comes with a price tag, and living the life you want and deserve comes with one too. You will live out of your comfort zone. You will always have to be humble, realize your mistakes and failures, and work on becoming better in everything you do. When everyone relaxes, you will be working. When they watch Netflix, you will be working. When they have it easy, you won't. When you sign up for the life you want and deserve, you are giving up on living in your comfort zone, and you are signing up for facing your fears, working hard, learning and growing, and becoming committed, hyper-focused and super-aware. It will be sweaty, messy, confusing, tiring, and really, really uncomfortable. But you will get to the life you want and deserve. If I could do it, so can you. So can anyone. I am not braver than you. I just wanted this really, really badly.

How badly do you want the life you want and deserve?

How much are you willing to pay?

Is it 1?
Is it 2?
Is it 3?
Is it 4?
Is it 5?
Is it 6?
Is it 7?
Is it 8?
Is it 9?
Is it 10?

GOOD IS NICE.

GO FOR GREAT.

CHAPTER EIGHT

GET IN THE DRIVER'S SEAT AND POWER THROUGH ADVERSITY

"You may not realize it when it happens, but a kick in the teeth may be the best thing in the world for you." –Walt Disney

When life hits you, it hits you hard. I am not going to lie to you and tell you to just power through. People say: when life gives you lemons, make≈lemonade. Well, easier said than done. Lemons can be pretty sour.

Every time life has knocked me down, I haven't felt like I wanted to 'power through adversity.' I just wanted to survive. When the economy collapsed in 2008, my husband lost his business, and we had literally no money at all, I just wanted to somehow pull through. I know you kind of expect me at this point to tell you the entire story about how I pulled through, but I am not going to do that. You know why? Because my challenges may be great for me, but maybe yours are greater. So we are going to skip the details, because the details don't matter. What matters is this. How much does it matter to you to pull through? What are you protecting? And what are you willing to do in order to protect it?

I was and still am willing to do everything to protect and take care of my family. Not that my kids don't give me a hard time. Don't think that anyone is putting me on a pedestal here. They laugh at me for forgetting pots on the stove and burning them. They complain that I am too busy (can you believe it?), and make comments about what I eat and how much I work out. They do love me, but over here in family land I am just Mom.

Will they ever understand that I am nervous before I go on stage, yet I do it anyway? That I am always unsure of everything I write, yet I write it anyway? That I would have loved to be just Mom, but that will never happen? I am out. Of. My. Comfort. Zone, and there is no way back.

When life happens, you can call it adversity or any bad name you want; but when life knocks your pearly white teeth off your face, you have two options as did I. You can give up and justify it to everyone else. Or you can fight for what matters to you the most, and in that fight you lead. People can join you or leave, but you won't care. When you make up your mind to power through, you become invincible. When something matters to you at a 10, you just don't care what you have to do, what other people think, sleep, comfort, what your mother says, what your best friend says. When you want something at a 10 you are Superman and Wonder Woman rolled together.

That is what happened to me.

I have asked myself many times what makes people resilient. How can we become even more resilient? Winters come. Storms come. Adversity hits. How can we become stronger, more resilient and more prepared?

There are four pillars to building your resilience. I will share all of them with you. I believe that you have all four of them within you. You just need to become more aware of them and work on them, like muscles in your body. The truth of the matter is that most of us realize sooner rather than later that we are far stronger than we think, far more resilient than we realize, a lot more resourceful than we give ourselves credit for, and capable of doing a lot more than we think we can. When something matters to you at a 10, all these things come together and work for you, and you overcome challenges. These are the three pillars that contribute to it.

Resilience pillar #1: Purpose

There is tremendous power in focusing on something greater than your immediate challenge.

Look at it this way. If you look at your challenge or pain as a stand-alone issue, it becomes very big. It defines and consumes you. You feel overwhelmed and can't see beyond your current pain.

But if you look at what is challenging you right now in the perspective of your overall purpose, all of a sudden it looks small and less intimidating.

Think of resilience as your chosen pair of glasses. It is a perspective. It is a state of mind in terms of how you process the things that are happening to you, and what meaning you give the events in your life.

Resilient people don't think in terms of blame or guilt. They are seeing things in a perspective that is greater than them. Blame is about avoiding responsibility, and guilt is about taking too much responsibility, often for things that are not really within your control. Both of those—guilt and blame—make you weak. Blame makes you weak because blame is about ego, assigning the responsibility to someone else. This is tempting because you may feel better for a moment, knowing someone else can be blamed for a problem. But this perspective takes you out of the driver's seat of a solution, because if someone else holds the blame and therefore the responsibility for the problem, what is there for you to do?

Guilt makes you just as weak, because you are overwhelming yourself with negative feelings about yourself: shame, anxiety, frustration and humiliation. Guilt is horrible for your self-worth and self-esteem. In order to be resilient you need to believe in yourself, and guilt works against you in that sense.

Here is what I want you to do in order to tackle your challenges without guilt or blame. With your resilience glasses on, I want you to think about something beyond yourself that matters to you very much. I want you to think about your 10.

I have shared with you in the past that my family has always been my 10 for me. This is not to say that your family should be your 10 for you. Your 10 can be anything. You owe no explanation to anyone. Your 10 is your 10, and any 10 is a wonder because it will give you strength and perspective, and that's all you need in order to be resilient.

Whenever you struggle, think of your 10. Tell yourself over and over again how much that thing matters to you and is dear to your heart. How passionate you are about it.

Research has shown that dedication to a worthy cause, or a belief in something greater than oneself—religiously or secularly—has a resilience-enhancing effect. It makes you strong. It makes you pivot. It makes you creative and flexible in your thinking.

It doesn't matter how other people become more resilient and what they do or not do. The only thing that matters right now is you.

You will become incredibly resilient when you focus your mind and heart on what matters to you the most. Your purpose. Your mission. Your 10.

"Out of suffering have emerged the strongest souls; the most massive characters are seared with scars." –Kahlil Gibran

Resilience pillar #2: Connection

You are stronger when you connect with others. You are also healthier the more you are connected. Research has consistently found that the ability to recover from hardship and move forward in a positive way is closely linked with the people in your life, and with the quality of your relationships with them.

I want you to think about your resilience the same way you think about your fitness. Some studies show that resiliency is not a life-long trait but something that fluctuates over time. One of the parameters that impact it is your social support network.

So while you may think about becoming more resilient as something you need to change or work on within yourself, research suggests that positive relationships and supportive environments have an important role to play.

You see, having good social relationships is clearly a winning strategy in life. It makes you healthier, both physically and mentally. It's not surprising, then, that social relationships also matter when it comes to resiliency, in part because they help you feel less stress when you are going through hard times.

Let me say it even more clearly: poor relationships with other people are more detrimental to your mental and physical health, and to your overall resilience, than smoking and obesity.

The reason for this is simple—when you have good relationships with other people, you experience less stress. When you do have stress, those relationships are comforting and help you manage your stress and feel better. If you have poor relationships with other people, it adds more stress to the stress you are already experiencing. By not getting along with other people, no matter how right you think you are, you are compromising your health and resilience.

If you are in trouble or going through a hard time, look around you. Who can you reach out to today who will make you feel better?

In other words, when you are going through a hard time, turn to the people around you. It takes a village to help each of its members bounce back from disaster. There is a village around you. All you need to do is just reach out.

> "Dare to reach out your hand into the darkness, to pull another hand into the light." –Norman B. Rice

Resilience pillar #3: Self-discipline

You may ask yourself how self-discipline makes you more resilient. The simple answer is that resilience is a form of self-discipline in itself. When you are working to become more resilient, you are working to discipline yourself in terms of your mindset.

Here are five ways you can train your mind to become more resilient:

1. Be Goal Oriented

By making a personal commitment to achieve a goal that is important to you (as always, focus on your 9s and 10s), and using self-discipline to hold yourself accountable, you're on your way to a mindset that looks more into crushing your goals and less into the obstacles in your way. In other words: when you don't have goals, every little hill feels like a mountain, because your focus is on the hill. When you have disciplined yourself to have clear goals, every mountain feels like a hill, because your focus is on the horizon.

2. Block Distractions

We live in a world full of distractions, and working from home augments them. Self-discipline helps you to focus on your goals. Disciplining yourself to block distractions and focus on your goals, and on the things that make you stronger, makes a big difference in building your resilience and success.

3. Create Winning Habits

Your winning habits make you stronger because they help you continue to behave in a way that contributes to your health and success, without having to think about it too much. If you have a winning habit of working out it will make you stronger, mentally and physically. If you have a winning habit to have a positive mindset it will make you stronger, mentally and physically. You are the culmination of your habits. Use your self-discipline to create (and keep!) the habits that will make you strong—mind, body and spirit.

4. Learn from Your Mistakes When They Happen

We all fail. We all make mistakes. But some of us let those define us and some of us don't. Which group do you want to discipline yourself to be a part of? Hint: the latter takes more self- discipline. Learning from your mistakes is all about holding yourself accountable but keeping yourself guilt-free. Guilt stands in the way of learning because it causes too much stress. There is no learning when there is acute stress. Discipline yourself to forgive yourself, and ask yourself, "How can I do this better going forward?"

5. Take Really Good Care of Yourself

For those of us who tend to put others before themselves (guilty!), discipline yourself to take really good care of yourself. Eat well. Exercise. Stay away from toxicity. Love yourself. Rest. Forgive yourself. Repeat as needed. <u>You are only strong when you are well taken care of.</u> No one will take care of you if you do not take care of yourself first. There is no resilience where there is no self-care. It is that simple.

"All successes begin with self-discipline. It starts with you." –Dwayne "The Rock" Johnson

ADVERSITY IS TEMPORARY.

LOVE IS ETERNAL.

PART 3

GET IN THE DRIVER'S SEAT OF YOUR LIFE

CHAPTER NINE

HOW TO BECOME THE PERSON YOU ARE MEANT TO BE

"The only person you are destined to become is the person you decide to be." –Ralph Waldo Emerson

Becoming the person you are meant to be is not something to leave to luck. Claiming the life you want and deserve is a matter of combining the power of 2 Second Decisions with the most cutting-edge science-based strategies to power through with a winning mindset, building winning habits and making winning everyday decisions in your life and career.

Many people have a vision of the person they feel they were meant to be. Others just have an unsatisfied feeling that they can do more. That they can be more. That they deserve more.

I want you to envision yourself five years from today. And I want you to envision BIG. Dream BIG. What are you envisioning? Who are you going to be five years from today? How will your life change? What do you want to be doing? How do you want to be living? How are you planning on growing and challenging yourself in the next five years?

There are two things that might stand in your way to become the person you want and deserve to be. Those are knowing how to, and you yourself. I'd like to address those now.

> YOU are your main obstacle in your way to becoming the person you want to be, can be and deserve to be.

When I say that you are your main obstacle, I mean that you might be behaving in the following ways:

- Sitting around waiting for the right time (spoiler alert: it's never going to be the right time)
- Waiting until you feel ready (guess what? You'll never feel ready)
- Seeing your mistakes as failures (this has got to change pronto. Your mistakes are your learning opportunities—they happened so that you can get better)
- Not anticipating the setbacks (there are always setbacks, there is no other way)
- Not making yourself and what matters to you a priority (huge mistake, we will talk about that in this chapter at length)
- Giving up (don't. This book is here to support you and give you the tools and courage to keep going all the way to becoming the person that you are mean to be and living the life that you want and deserve.)

Let's also talk about not knowing HOW to become the person you are meant to be. This part is really important and we are going to fix it here with this book. How on Earth are you supposed to know how to be successful and maximize your potential, if you were not lucky enough to be able to witness someone in your life, such as a parent or a role model, actually do it? Schools do not teach success that way. Schools teach success in the form of grades, sports, and being a good member of society, and I respect that. But schools do not teach you how to negotiate, how to keep yourself mentally healthy, how to assess yourself, how to handle adversity, how to forgive, how to handle uncertainty, and how to learn from failure. Schools don't teach you how to make everyday winning decisions quickly and effectively. It may be that you want to become the person you are meant to be, but you just don't know how.

When I discovered 2 Second Decisions I was at that exact intersection in my own life. I had the unsettling feeling of being unsatisfied with my life and career, and with who I was and where I was at the time. Like many people, I knew what I didn't want, and came to find out after a while what I did want. I just had no idea how to get there, how to overcome the obstacles, how to believe in myself, and how to respect my goals and my vision of my future no matter what.

What I have learned through my journey, I am going to share with you. In this chapter we will talk about how to build and maintain a winning mindset, how to build the kind of habits that push you forward, how to set the goals that are the right ones for you (and for you only), how to build the kind of resilience that will allow you to power through anything, and how to get along with anyone, literally anyone, in your personal and professional life.

Let's start.

How to build and maintain a winning mindset

You can massively change your life by changing your mindset. Mindset is probably the most important asset you have. It is also your most powerful tool, if you use it the right way.

If you analyze the lives of some of the most successful people in the world, you will realize that their success is not because they had it easy.

Larry King filed for bankruptcy the very same year he started a 25-year career as one of the most popular radio and television hosts in America.

Tony Robbins grew up with a mother who has been described as an abusive alcoholic and pill addict. He had a series of stepfathers and left his family to start life on his own, after his mother chased him out of their house with a knife.

Jim Carrey's family lost everything and lived in a van.

Richard Branson has dyslexia and got bad grades at school.

Stephen King's first novel was rejected 30 times.

Oprah Winfrey gave birth at age 14 and lost her child. She was molested by her uncle, cousin and a family friend.

Simon Cowell had a failed record company.

Charlize Theron witnessed her mother kill her alcoholic father in an act of self-defense.

All of these people came from great adversity. They came from pain, from difficulty, and from huge challenges. They had every reason in the world not to pull through, but they did. Big time. Why?

The answer may sound overly simplistic, but it has all of the wisdom in the world in it.

Mindset.

These people, as well as many everyday people, have developed a certain mindset that made them win.

Having a winning mindset is a massively distinguishing factor, one that separates those who live the life they want and deserve from those who stay stuck.

Your mindset determines your attitude in every given situation. I want you to think of your mindset as if you have in front of you right now two pairs of eyeglasses to choose from, green and red. The green glasses stand for a positive mindset. Through them you see challenges as opportunities, and failure as a step toward getting better and wiser. These green glasses tell you—GO! Go on and don't stop until you get to the life you want and deserve, until you become the person you were meant to become.

The red glasses stand for a negative mindset. Through them you see that getting out of your comfort zone is scary. Through the red glasses, risk feels like a potential embarrassment. Failure feels like you are the failure. These red glasses stop you from making progress. They keep you stuck.

Which glasses do you choose to use?

What happened to you in life in the past, or what is happening to you right now, does not define you. It is your interpretation of what is happening that defines you, your life and your future. The good news is that **your interpretation of your life's challenges is a matter of mindset, and your mindset is a matter of choice.**

You have the power to choose how to act in every area of your life, no matter what you are dealing with. You are the product of the choices you make: how you manage your time, how you earn money, if you eat that salad for lunch or not. In order to take action in your life, you first need to adopt a winning mindset. You need to put your green glasses on, and break your red glasses and throw them in the trash. No more.

You are strong, you are capable, and you are far more powerful than you can even imagine. As long as you have your green glasses with you and know how to make 2 Second Decisions, I know you will win.

How to build the kind of habits that push you forward

Before we talk about building winning habits that push you forward, I want you to understand how habits work in the human mind. Once you understand that, you will understand that the art and science of creating winning habits will get you on track to the life you want and deserve.

I want you to think of habits like beaten paths in the forest. I want you to envision those beaten paths in your mind. I want you to actually see them. Your habits create neural pathways in your brain.

Neural pathways are the connections between your brain's neurons. Specific neurons will fire based on what we are asking our brains to do, and similarly the pathways we have access to are based on the connections we've created by specific neurons talking to each other.

New neural pathways are established through habits you repeat. The more you repeat the action, the more you strengthen the neural pathway, which means the more 'beaten paths' you are dealing with in your brain. Once you have created a new neural pathway, which means that you have created a new (and winning!) habit, it's simply up to you to maintain it. Not using a pathway, which happens when you don't practice the new habit, weakens its connection. It's still there, it's just not as easy to walk on as it used to be.

Because your brain is very costly to your body in terms of energy (it spends about 20% of your bodily energy), it simply prefers not to spend any more energy on adopting new habits. For that reason, <u>it will always try to take the path of least resistance—the beaten path of an already established habit.</u>

When your brain is repeating the beaten path of a habit, you are on autopilot. It doesn't need to use much energy because it doesn't need to engage the prefrontal cortex, the executive part of the brain in charge of making decisions. The prefrontal cortex requires larger amounts of energy than the rest of the brain, and is used when you learn new behaviors and focus on new things. When the prefrontal cortex is not engaged, you are slipping back into old habits, both the good ones and the bad.

2 Second Decisions will change your life because they will enable you to make winning decisions in the quickest and most effective way, without costing the prefrontal cortex too much energy. Even then, you cannot use 2 Second Decisions for each one of the 35,000 decisions you make every day. You goal is to automate winning habits in order to free your brain to make new winning decisions. If you spend your brain's energy on deciding whether to work out or not, to eat a salad for lunch or not, to go to the gym or not, you are wasting your brain's energy on things that can be automated. Once you get those things into your routine as a habit, they become beaten paths of neural pathways in your brain, and they will happen on autopilot without even thinking. Then, and only then, can you use 2 Second Decisions for new winning decisions that will push you forward.

How to set the goals that are the right goals for you (and you only)

I want you to stop and think how much of your life is shaped by living up to the expectations of others. We all struggle with it in some way. As children your parents established rules for how you should behave. When you went to school, your teachers told you what was expected. If you did not follow what was expected, you could face not being allowed to go up to the next grade. It takes time as an adult to learn to develop your own expectations, both of yourself and of others.

This is far more common than you think. You unconsciously take on other people's wishes for you. It can be very hard to tell the difference between what you want for yourself and something that your mother or your best friend thinks is best for you. The people around you may want nothing but the best for you, and they may be right or not—that's beside the point. The real problem starts when you adopt other people's goals for you without checking with yourself if that is what you actually want.

Sometimes it's hard to tell where your dreams end and someone else's starts. When someone asks 'how are you?' and you answer them fully and honestly, you may find yourself in a situation where they urge you to dump your friend, divorce your husband or quit your job. I am not telling you not to ignore the people in your life who love you. But I am telling you to always check the things they say against what you really want, and what matters to you the most.

I want you to leave room in your mind for what you want, for what matters to you the most. I also want you to understand how powerful it is when you define a goal for yourself that means a lot to you, something you are passionate about. Goal setting literally changes the structure of your brain so that it is optimized to achieve that goal.

If you strongly desire a goal, your brain will perceive obstacles as less significant than they might otherwise appear. That means when you know what you want and you define it to yourself, you know deep in your heart that you are aligned with what matters to you the most, and you will become more resilient no matter what comes your way. I will talk about that more in the next chapter; but in the meantime, I cannot stress this enough, that you live this life for you. Always be checking in with yourself: What do I want? What matters the most to me?

How to build the kind of resilience that will allow you to power through anything

Resilience will not make your problems go away, but it will give you the strength to power through a setback in your life, or a major challenge such as the death of a loved one, the loss of your job, or dealing with an illness or disaster. What resilience gives you is the perspective to see beyond the present challenge, the hope to imagine a better future, and the coping mechanisms to handle adversity, without turning to numbing activities like substance abuse or becoming completely overwhelmed.

The power behind resilience is first and foremost your ability to see yourself as someone who is able to power through adversity. In other words, you seeing yourself as a strong person.

2 Second Decisions are there to give you an immediate sense of control over your life. Generally, resilient people tend to have what psychologists call an internal locus of control, which means they feel they control their own destiny, rather than their fate being largely determined by external forces. They tend to be happier, less depressed, and less stressed.

External events in your life are out of your control, that's true. But how you perceive yourself within the situation makes a huge difference. Do you feel in control or out of control? Do you feel powerful or powerless?

Becoming resilient is not a mysterious skill, but rather a healthy choice and lifestyle. When adversity comes your way, don't tell yourself 'why me?' Don't ask yourself 'why am I always out of luck?' Don't let yourself feel like a victim or feel sorry for yourself. Take these three steps instead:

1. Winning Mindset: TELL yourself that this is a lesson. Ask yourself what you can learn from this.
2. Winning Decisions: DECIDE to take action. Make 2 Second Decisions to shift from passive reaction to actions that will make you feel better. Decide to take the position of managing the situation rather than being managed by it.
3. Winning Actions: ACT. Being passive and feeling helpless are the cancer of resilience. You are the leader of your own life. You are the master and the manager. Manage the situation and take action. Do not be passively managed by it.

WHAT YOU BELIEVE ABOUT
YOURSELF AND WHAT YOU
CAN ACCOMPLISH IS THE
STRONGEST FORCE IN YOUR LIFE.

CHAPTER TEN

STOP LIVING OTHER PEOPLE'S EXPECTATIONS

"Your time is limited, so don't waste it living someone else's life." –Steve Jobs

Let's face it. Living other people's expectations means compromising who you really are and what you really want. Do you sometimes feel you don't like your life? Do you sometimes get a feeling, deep inside, that you are a bit off on how you do things? That something is missing or just doesn't feel right?

If you have that feeling about your life, it is because somehow you have allowed other people to influence or determine your choices, and you are trying to please them and whatever they expect of you.

You are not alone. Expectations are a part of our upbringing and how we process information. In this chapter, I will teach you **how to live alongside expectations, but change your relationship with them.**

Let's start by defining what expectations are and why they are so deceiving.

You are Conditioned to Live by Expectations

The human mind is conditioned to live by expectations—of life, of other people, of yourself, of what you think is going to happen next—to help you manage all the information you are exposed to every day. Those expectations **help you make decisions in an environment of uncertainty, based on previous patterns of things that happened before.**

When you stand at a red light, you know the light will eventually turn green. You expect it because you have experienced it before, many times. When the winter is harsh, you expect the cold to go away and you expect spring to come, based on the changing seasons you have experienced before. This way you don't worry about having to stand there at the red light forever, or being cooped up inside for the rest of your life.

Expectations make you feel more emotionally stable, because they help you feel prepared for things that might happen. In that sense, **expectations are good for you, as long as they are your own.**

The people around you perceive you in a certain way, and therefore have certain expectations of you. But the way other people perceive you is not you; it is a subjective image of you that they have created in their mind. It is subjective because these people are not you. They are just trying to process a lot of information about you, and based on that make assumptions and create expectations based on things they know about other people from past experiences.

Other people's expectations of you are based on the image they have of you.

You Find Yourself Really Caring About What Other People Think About You

I want you to think of the idea of caring what other people think about you as something ancient, archaic, buried in an old closet that smells like mothballs. Here is why.

One of the most common mind fallacies we have is the idea that what other people think about us really matters. This has ancient roots because it comes from a time in which our primal ancestors shared the planet with saber-toothed tigers, and no one wanted to be left behind. Group acceptance was critical to survival.

This ancient notion that once saved lives has become in modern life the opposite. It is the fear of not being accepted that causes people to compromise who they are and who they can grow into, and makes them live other people's expectations instead of their own lives to the fullest.

In looking out, rather than within, our sense of self and sense of confidence become compromised. You cannot talk about empowerment as long as you are co-dependent on oversharing on social media, seeking approval and craving compliments online or in real life. If you are doing that, stop. You are fueling a false self, playing a role and acting out of a fear of not being accepted.

The day you stop caring about what other people think, and trust your own 2 Second Decisions, is the day you start winning at life. As long as you care what other people think, you are in the backseat of your own life. The day you stop caring what other people think, and start trusting your own instincts and decisions, even if you take wrong turns sometimes, is the day you are in the driver's seat and in control of where your life is going.

How You Manage Other People's Expectations is Your Master Key for Getting in the Driver's Seat of Your Life

The fact that other people have expectations of you is normal. The real question on the table is how you manage other people's expectations. Or in other words: **what your relationship is with other people's expectations, and how this impacts your life.**

There is a concern with you living other people's expectations, and you need to be aware of it. Every time you are following other people's expectations, you are dropping the ball on being the leader of your own life. You are getting out of the driver's seat of your life and leaving it to someone else to take the lead.

Possible reasons for letting someone else and their expectations of you get in the driver's seat of your life include:

- You do not trust yourself (you assume that they—your parents, your friends, your coworkers—know better than you)
- You are afraid of failure (this way, if you fail you can blame them)
- You think you are not good at making decisions and leave it to others (this book puts an end to that)
- You are used to other people taking the lead on decisions for you

This book is all about getting in the driver's seat of your life, but you cannot do so as long as you let other people's expectations take the lead. The honest truth is that people-pleasing kills success. Think of it as a subconscious habit that needs to stop. **Stop living your life for the sole purpose of making other people happy.** Those other people should live their lives being happy for themselves! Being in the driver's seat of your life, work, future and choices is your BIRTHRIGHT.

It took me many years to come to terms with the fact that when I am in the driver's seat and take a leadership position, not everyone is happy with me. I spent so much energy trying to walk the fine line of being approved, and felt that being too controversial is not "nice." For many years I wanted to be nice, and I wanted to be approved of by as many people in my life as possible.

I want to talk about the need for approval and I want to talk about the need to be nice, because throwing those out the window is exactly what gets you in the driver's seat of your life, work and future. I stopped craving approval and got myself in the driver's seat of my life with 2 Second Decisions because I got clear and confident with all decisions I make in my life. And you can use 2 Second Decisions in the exact same way, every time you feel you are slipping away from the driver's seat of your life to the passenger seat, which is when you give up leadership of your life and slip into following other people's expectations.

> By trying to please everyone, you please no one— yourself included.

Signs of People-Pleasing to Watch Out for

I want you to read these people-pleasing behaviors and see if you are recognizing any of these in your life. One of the most common pitfalls is to be geared toward pleasing others but seeing yourself as nice and kind. I am not telling you not to be nice and kind, but I am definitely telling you that you might have forgotten to be nice and kind to yourself. Check if you recognize yourself in any of the following.

You have low self-esteem

Do you actually feel confident about yourself? People-pleasers have low self-esteem and derive their sense of esteem from the approval of others. You may believe that people only care about you when you bring value—when you are helpful, when you give 110% of yourself, when you go above and beyond for the other person. Sound familiar?

You need other people to really like you

Let's look at the opposite option here: can you handle not being liked? People-pleasers really dread rejection. Check if the things you do and the choices you make are aimed at being liked. You may also have a need for other people to really need you. In your subconscious you feel that this way, even if they don't like you, you will not be rejected.

You have a hard time saying 'no'

Saying yes when deep inside you actually want to say no is literally the opposite of leadership of your own life. You may do this because you dread the reaction. It seems easier just to say yes and deal with the consequences. It seems like a safer option—no conflict, no risk of being rejected, even if you don't really feel like doing the thing you said yes to, and don't feel it was the right choice for you. This is a pattern that causes nothing but problems, because it teaches the people around you that their needs come before yours. You will be amazed how much more control you will have over your life, work and future just by learning how to say no. We will talk about saying no and setting boundaries at length in the next chapter.

You apologize even when you know it is not your fault

Are you finding yourself apologizing just to avoid an argument? Taking the blame for something you really should not apologize for happens because you are catering to someone else's need for you to apologize, so that they can avoid taking responsibility. You are squashing your sense of self if you do that, and you are also doing a disservice to the other person, because you are teaching them that they can get away with not being accountable. I actually used to do that myself. I hate arguments so much that I used to apologize—to my mom, to my husband—just to stop arguing. It took me years to understand how short-sighted I was being in doing that, supposedly solving an argument in the short run (everybody is happy, the problem is solved, I apologized) but creating huge damage in the long run. My resentment grew, because I was teaching others to disrespect my opinions and boundaries, and I compromised my sense of self. I am proud to say that there is no chance in a million years of me doing that again. That clarity of who you are, what you want, and what matters to you the most, that you gain by using 2 Second Decisions, and the growing sense of self-confidence and belief in yourself that come with it, get you in the driver's seat of your life.

You are quick to agree and conform

Agreeing and conforming can sometimes seem like the quickest way to win the approval of others. Do you find yourself quick to say 'great idea!' or 'fantastic plan,' even when you don't really think that? It is time for you to stop going along with something that doesn't sit right with you, because you are doing a disservice to yourself and others. If something doesn't sit right with you, don't say it's a great idea. If you need time to think, say, "I am not sure. I need to think about it." If you have questions, ask them. And if something doesn't sit right with you, speak up.

You struggle with authenticity

When you are busy pleasing others, you have a hard time recognizing your own feelings. The truth is that the more you push your own feelings under the rug, the less authentic you become, both with yourself and others. I used to have a very hard time expressing how I feel. I was so busy masking it that I became unclear even to myself about how I feel and what matters to me the most. If you struggle with recognizing and verbalizing your own feelings, this is a warning sign for you. I want you to keep this in mind when you read the coming chapters "How to Have the Courage to be Yourself" and "Beat Fear." There is no worse feeling than trying to be any less than who you are. There is no greater feeling of relief than being authentic to who you are. I know because I have been there.

You just give and give

Don't get me wrong, giving is a beautiful thing. The question is why you give. For those of us who over-give, you are doing so with the hope that people reciprocate with the acceptance and love you need. Learn to give to yourself, not just others. And train yourself to expect to accept gladly. Love and acceptance that depend on over-giving are short-lived, and they are driven by fear.

You have a hard time handling conflict and arguments

This one hits home for me because I still struggle to overcome it. I hate conflict, especially with the people I love, and have to force myself to confront issues when needed. So here is what I have learned: by all means, confront. Just learn how to do it. As long as you are respectful and calm, you can confront any issue you want if it really matters to you, 0 to 10. The older I've gotten, the better I've gotten at controlling my temper. Once you can do that, you can have any conflicts you want and confront any issue. Self-control leads to a sense of empowerment and empowerment beats fear.

Are you seeking external or internal validation?

When you seek external validation, you need compliments to feel worthy.

When you rely on internal validation you need no one but yourself to know your worth.

One of the first ways to overcome a behavior is to first identify the "why" behind it.

Human beings feel a deep compulsion to be part of a tribe. It's a very primal need to feel accepted by others, because when we're accepted that means we get to stay in the tribe. Which back in the day—like way, way back in the day—meant surviving.

Of course, with the rise of billions more humans, we no longer need the approval of everyone to survive and thrive. **But that fear of being left out is so ingrained in our minds, it's not easy to shake. It's simply the way your mind keeps you safe.**

Since the need for validation is engrained in you, you cannot change it. What you can do is change where that validation is coming from. That means that you are going to shift from craving external validation—relying on compliments and social-media likes to feel good about yourself—to internal validation—encouraging yourself, prioritizing your needs, and taking the lead of your own decisions.

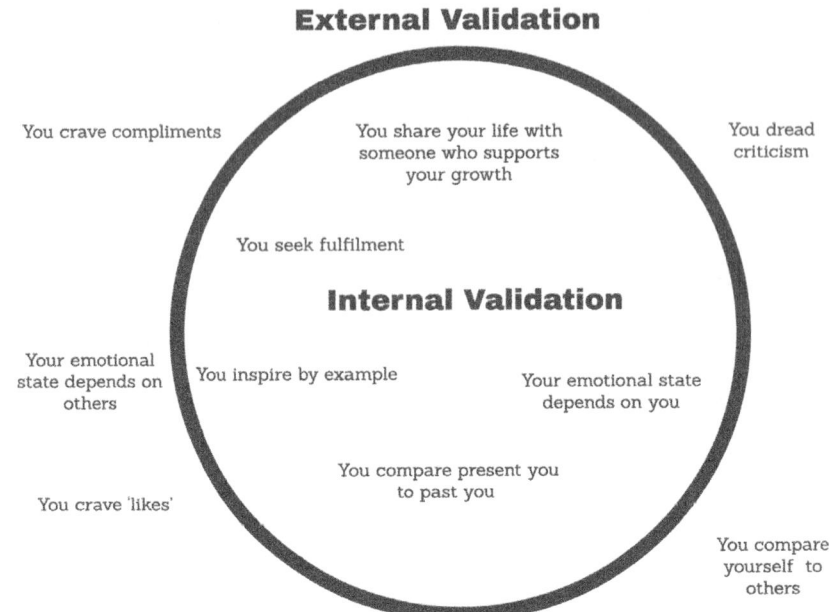

External Validation

You crave compliments

You share your life with
someone who supports
your growth

You dread
criticism

You seek fulfilment

Internal Validation

Your emotional
state depends on
others

You inspire by example

Your emotional state
depends on you

You compare present you
to past you

You crave 'likes'

You compare
yourself to
others

> Frustration is the gap between what people expect of you and who you are.

Get in the driver's seat. You are the leader of your own life, and leaders do not engage in seeking likes and approval. They take the lead and risk disapproval if they are confident that they are making the right decision, which is why 2 Second Decisions is your best ally for becoming confident about your choices, instead of relying on others to make them for you. Speak up. Take risks. Teach yourself that taking the lead and making decisions means you are in control of your life. If someone doesn't like that, it means nothing but that you have just dared to get in the driver's seat of your life. Brené Brown says in her book *Dare to Lead*, "*We fail the minute we let someone else define success for us.*"

I want you to use 2 Second Decisions to stop being afraid. To take the lead on your life and to stop relying on others.

THERE WILL ALWAYS BE
SOMEONE WHO DOESN'T SEE
HOW AMAZING YOU ARE.

BUT AT THE END OF THE
DAY—WHO CARES?

CHAPTER ELEVEN

START SAYING NO WITHOUT FEELING BAD ABOUT IT

*"The art of leadership is saying no, not saying yes.
It is very easy to say yes."* –Tony Blair

"No" is the one of the shortest words in the English language, and yet one of the hardest words to say. A big mistake people make is thinking that saying no makes them selfish, rude or unkind. Think back to when you were a kid, and how many times you easily said no then. Why has it become so hard to say it now when you are an adult?

As a child you soon learn that saying no to your parents, your grandma or your teacher means you'll be lectured or punished for being rude. Parents and teachers tend to like the idea of kids who are easy and agreeable, and really struggle with strong-willed kids who do not listen… or worse, argue. (I know this firsthand; I was the kid who always argued, and now as a parent I have my own kid who should have the word "no" as his middle name. He eventually ended up captain of varsity debate, but having all these debates at home over every little thing drove me nuts, just like it did to the adults around me when I was a kid.)

Unfortunately, in the process of shifting from being a child—where conforming to adults make you a 'good kid'—to adulthood, where you are expected to know how to set limits and know your boundaries, saying no for many adults is still associated with guilt, shame, and fear of being alone or abandoned.

If you are having a hard time saying no and setting boundaries, this comes with a very high price tag for you. You end up finding yourself in situations where you have too many things to do, but most of them don't have real value for you and your life. In other words, because you have a hard time saying no, you are stuck wasting your time on things that don't really matter for your life, work and future, all kinds of 2s and 1s that don't really matter to you that much, and just happened because you couldn't say no and now don't have enough time or energy for your 9s and your 10s. This causes you unnecessary stress, wastes your time, and makes your days and your life so much harder, for no good reason.

So why do you do this to yourself? There are several reasons:

You want to help: Not every instance of helping someone is an act of kindness, generosity and empathy. In some cases it is, and that's a wonderful thing. But in other cases, you are doing something that is not aligned with what you can give or do at that moment. Helping someone else at the expense of causing yourself a high level of stress is an act of self-abuse, because now you don't have enough money, time or energy for yourself. Helping someone is a wonderful thing, as long as you are also taking your own well-being into account.

You are afraid you will be rejected: Because you are associating saying yes to being loved from back in your childhood, you are fearful of saying no. Failing to set boundaries doesn't guarantee love. It guarantees exhaustion and resentment.

You feel guilty about saying no: You feel guilty when you think you did something wrong. And you associate saying no with doing something that is not nice and acceptable. You are just as important as other people. When you say yes when you should be saying no, you are not only hurting yourself and but also teaching others to disrespect you and your boundaries.

You are tired and worn out: This one is a vicious cycle. Because you are preconditioned during childhood to associate conforming with rewards, you need to be focused and mindful as an adult in order to do the opposite—set boundaries and say no when you need to. If you are too tired and worn out, you'll revert back to what you are preconditioned to do. You'll say yes without even thinking it through, and then regret it. In doing that, you have overburdened yourself and now you are more tired and worn out than before. And the vicious cycle goes on.

> "In order to thrive and be successful, you have to be able to set boundaries." –Oprah Winfrey

Learning how to say no is like learning how to ride a bike. At first you are bound to fail and scratch your knees; but once you get really good at it, you are in for a completely new kind of way of navigating the world around you. You cannot be successful if you don't know how to say no. So those days of saying yes when you actually mean no, or saying yes without thinking it through and then miserably regretting it, are gone.

This is where 2 Second Decisions come into play—you don't have to think about it too much. All you have to do is to get out your own head and give it a number.

How right is this for me to do this?

Is it 1?
Is it 2?
Is it 3?
Is it 4?

Is it 5?

Is it 6?

Is it 7?

Is it 8?

Is it 9?

Is it 10?

Once you've got out of your head and give it a number, you will have clarity with yourself if you are in no or yes territory.

Here is what you should do next: **If your number is 1–4, Say NO. Here is how.**

There is one rule of thumb for saying no effectively—just say it. Don't apologize. You don't have to explain, and there is no need to make any excuses. So before we talk about tips and strategies and dos and don'ts, understand this: there is no right or wrong way to say no. The only thing that is wrong is saying yes instead.

To get really good at following that one rule of thumb, here are some things to do…and some things to avoid.

Do blame something objective

Blaming something objective, such as your workload or your schedule, makes your no completely non-personal. It is circumstance-based and, as such, it is out of your control. People have a hard time accepting a 'no' when they perceive it as personal, but they actually have a very easy time accepting a 'no' when it is based on circumstances. The people who ask for your time, attention, focus and money may not realize what situation they are putting you in, or they may care more about what they want than about how that impacts you.

The easiest way to deal with these people, without having a relationship with them go completely sour, is to decide you live by clear principles and define to yourself what those are. For example: "I cannot be interrupted when I am at work unless it is an emergency." It's easier to make decisions if you are clear with yourself on what your policy is (in other words, what your boundaries are), and people are more likely to respect your responses.

Also, there's less chance of someone feeling personally rejected if it's clear this is a "rule" you live by consistently.

Do be assertive

The secret of being assertive when you say no lies in being convinced yourself. For that you have the 2 Second Decisions. Once you have the clarity that something is wrong for you, your mind will make it easier for you to be assertive because you will not experience doubt. Now, let's get something straight. Saying no is going to be uncomfortable. There is no way around it. You don't know what the outcome is going to be, and you don't know if the other person is going to personally attack you. In the chapter "Stop Living Other People's Expectations" we talked about the fact that humans have a fundamental need to belong, that comes from survival in primal times being dependent on being part of a group. For that reason, we are strongly motivated to remain in good standing with the people around us, because we fear exclusion. The fear of being excluded is perceived in your brain as a threat and triggers your "fight or flight" response.

But here is the thing. Once you get out of your own head and give a number to how right it is to say yes, you have the clarity of what is right for you. In doing that, you are shifting your brain from fight or flight to clarity and calm. You being assertive means that you are demonstrating the heathy confidence to stand up for yourself, while still respecting the rights of others. This means you are neither passive nor aggressive. You are direct, honest and clear in what you are saying, which you can only do when you are calm and in control.

Don't be aggressive and say:

"Are you deaf? I said no!"

Or, *"Not in a million years!"*

Or even, *"What makes you think I would want to do that?"*

Don't be passive and say:

"Okay, I'll do it…this time."

Or, *"Hmm, maybe."*

Don't be passive aggressive and say:

"Sure, fine, whatever."

Or, *"Do I really have a choice?"*

Or, *"I'll get back to you about it"* and never do.

Instead say:

"Normally I would say yes, but I am already committed to something else."

Or, *"I need to decline, but I do hope you'll keep me in mind for the future."*

Or, *"While I would love to do that for you, I can't right now. I hope you understand."*

Do offer an alternative

This is best for when you truly believe the request is worth looking into again in the future. If you're absolutely sure this is something you want to consider again, offer to reschedule at a better time when you can devote your full attention. Say something like, "I can't today. How about [insert new schedule]?"

Do start with a positive, then proceed to a boundary

Start on a positive note by sincerely complimenting or thanking the person for thinking of you. You can then follow it up with an honest reason why you can't accept the request or why you won't be able to make it to this engagement. For example, "The idea sounds great! It's just that…"

Don't make excuses

Excuses are very easy to see through, and they make both you and the other person uncomfortable. Think about it: excuses are something you typically go for if you did something wrong. If you are leaning towards making excuses when you say no, it shows that you are still feeling you are doing something wrong, when in fact you are doing something right. Once you have made a 2 Second Decision to decline, know that you are doing the right thing and stand behind your decision. Spare the other person and yourself the need to keep a straight face through unnecessary excuses.

Don't avoid

The essence of successfully saying no and setting boundaries is respect, both to yourself and to the other person. For that reason, you should always be direct and honest, even if you are really worried about the consequences of saying no. I consider avoiding to be the worst form of disrespect. <u>Honest and direct communication respects both you and the other person,</u> and leaves room for both of you to feel respected and dignified.

Don't attack, blame or shame

Some people get so stressed out by a situation of having to say no that they end up attacking the other person, because they feel frustrated and angry by being in a situation that causes them stress and discomfort. That's unfair to the other person. It's okay for people to ask you to do things. It's also okay for people to try to move your boundaries. It's normal. What is not okay is to cave in when you don't want to, or attack for no reason. Train yourself to be calm and assertive and not only will you be proud of yourself, but the other person will respect you and your boundaries.

> "Very successful people say no to almost everything." –Warren Buffet

If your number is 5-8, say no to a mindless yes. Postpone your answer.

A 5 to 8 signals to you that you don't know what to do, and you need more time to process. That in itself is a winning decision. Maybe you are too tired or busy to think right now. Maybe you need more information. I have learned over the years to use 2 Second Decisions not just in order to decide, but also in order to not decide.

<u>The value of 2 Second Decisions is not in making a decision no matter what. It is in making a **mindful** decision no matter what.</u> If the number you have given yourself says you are not even sure what your answer is, then postpone your answer, because delaying is better than a mindless yes or a careless no.

You could say:

"I need more time to process."

"I need to think about it."

"Let me sleep on it."

"I am too tired/distracted/busy right now. Let's talk at…"

But make sure not to turn postponing into avoiding. That is not the idea here. Be clear with the other person in terms of when you'll touch base again, and make sure to ask yourself again when you are more calm, rested and relaxed. "0 to 10, how right is this for me to do?" If you are still getting a middle-of-the-road answer, break it down into smaller questions in order to get clearer with yourself:

How likely am I to regret this?

How much of a pattern is this?

To what extent is the agenda here to use me?

> "The art of leadership is saying no, not saying yes. Saying yes is very easy." –Tony Blair

If your number is 9-10, Say YES

The rule of thumb for when to say yes is when it feels right to you. Period. Deep inside, you know what you want to do. 2 Second Decisions are there to help bring it to your awareness.

Saying yes to something that is right for you means that it is within the scope of what you can handle and what you feel is okay. The chart below demonstrates the three parameters of a healthy yes:

THE 3 PARAMETERS OF A HEALTHY YES

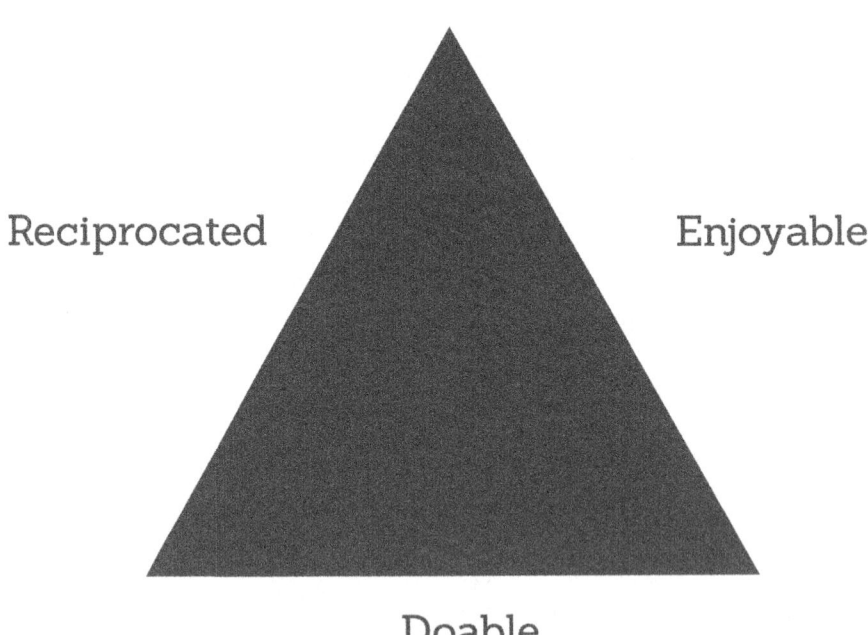

Reciprocated   Enjoyable

Doable

A healthy yes is **doable**: it does not deplete your resources and leave you on empty or low, as far as your time, money, energy and focus.

A healthy yes is **enjoyable**: you get pleasure from responding positively, and do not feel resentful or used.

A healthy yes is **reciprocated**: you are not the only one who makes an effort, and this is a two ways relationship.

> "You must trust the small voice inside you that tells you exactly what to say, what to decide."
> –Ingrid Bergman

THE SECRET TO SUCCESS AND HAPPINESS IS SIMPLE: LEARN TO LIVE AT PEACE WITH SETTING BOUNDARIES AND SAYING NO.

CHAPTER TWELVE

FREE YOURSELF FROM ANXIETY AND BEING OVERWHELMED

"You are not a mess. You are a feeling person in a messy world." –Glennon Doyle

Anxiety and Being Overwhelmed Happen. Here is Why

Anxiety is what happens when your worry is in the driver's seat of your life. Your thoughts of worry are spiraling out of control, and you feel powerless and weak. You may feel that you are the only one struggling while everyone else is normal.

I say, forget normal. Normal doesn't exist. Everyone feels anxious and overwhelmed at some point and to some extent. Studies show that anxiety is the #1 most common mental health problem in America, affecting one out of five people. If you experience more anxiety than you can handle, and you feel it is standing in your way of the life you want and deserve, you are not alone and this is certainly not your fault. Scientists have been able to isolate a number of genes associated with anxiety. In fact it is genetic, so if one of your parents or siblings has anxiety, you are four times more likely to experience it too.

There is a difference between experiencing episodes of anxiety and having an anxiety disorder. Anxiety is a term that many people use in different contexts. People might say 'I feel anxious' or 'this is causing me anxiety,' which is a normal part of life, but this is different from people with anxiety disorders who have intense, excessive and persistent fear and worry about everyday situations. People with anxiety disorders have repeated episodes of sudden intense fear that peak within minutes, known as panic attacks.

These feelings of anxiety and panic interfere with daily activities, are difficult to control, are out of proportion to the actual danger, and can last a long time. People with anxiety disorders typically avoid places or situations to prevent these feelings. Experiencing panic attacks and living with anxiety disorders require therapy and, in many cases, medication. If you are experiencing anxiety that is persistent and not occasional, one of your tools for getting in the driver's seat of your life is to reach out to a professional and get the help you need. If you haven't done that already, take the first step today and make that call. If you are working with someone and it is not helping you, reach out to another professional. Having an anxiety disorder is not your fault. There is nothing wrong with you.

There is so much pain in the world about anxiety, and so much pain around people feeling overwhelmed. I'd like to define with you what anxiety and being overwhelmed is, look with you at why they happen, and give you the tools to free yourself from both of them, so that you can get in the driver's seat of your life, work and courage. You cannot be in the driver's seat when anxiety controls you and when you feel overwhelmed. You have to regain control.

The worst part of anxiety is that it is debilitating and avoidance based. When you are anxious over a problem, you are running it over and over in your head. You are stuck in a cycle of thoughts and it feels like there is no one there to reach out and pull you out of that cycle of more and more worry.

You may also use the term 'overwhelmed' often. Being overwhelmed means that everything just feels like too much. When you say you are overwhelmed you are basically saying 'I don't believe I can manage this.' If you feel that you can identify why you are overwhelmed, it makes it easier, because we all have limits over what we can and can't manage, in terms of our time and energy. Maybe you have too much work to do, or people around you make your life challenging. In other cases, you may not be able to even identify why you are feeling overwhelmed. Something small happened, like the dishwasher broke, and all of a sudden you lose it.

The opposite of anxiety is action. Here is how you can help yourself

Whether your anxiety is a disorder or consists of isolated events like mine, whether it is severe or just happens sometimes, I want you to understand the two polarities that you are working with here:

Anxiety	⟷	Getting in the driver's seat of your life
Debilitating		Empowering
Confusing		Getting clear on what matters to you the most
No action		Taking action

2 Second Decisions are all about reclaiming control and taking action. Anxiety is all about avoidance and the sense of feeling powerless.

Here is how anxiety makes you weak and creates a cycle:

THE CYCLE OF ANXIOUS THOUGHTS

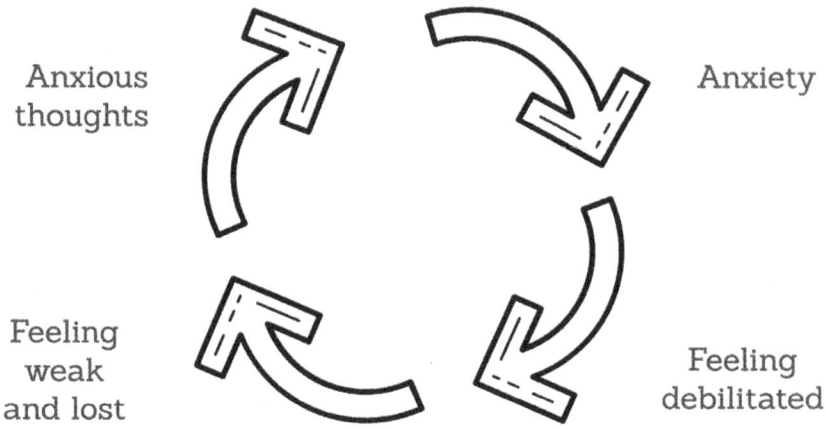

Anxious thoughts

Anxiety

Feeling weak and lost

Feeling debilitated

What are you missing out on because of anxiety? The relationships you want? The career you deserve? Being the leader or parent that you can and should be?

There are two steps for you to feel better. The first handles the short term and the second builds your long-term resilience and strength. They both revolve around 2 Second Decisions and this is how they work.

Step 1 to combat a cycle of anxiety: Get in the driver's seat and take action

Procrastinating, being passive aggressive, and dealing with rumination (continuously thinking the same thoughts) are all unhealthy coping mechanisms to things that make you anxious. By choosing to procrastinate, you are avoiding what makes you anxious (just to find out that this is making you even more anxious). By being passive aggressive you are avoiding a conflict or a direct communication (just to find out that this only makes things much worse). By ruminating, you are staying stuck in your own dark thoughts, while taking no real action for those thoughts to stop haunting you.

This is called avoidance coping—trying to avoid what stresses you out instead of dealing with it—and it always makes things worse.

We are in the business of stress management. We are in the business of regaining control. We are not in the business of running away from problems by avoiding them. Here is why when you procrastinate, engage in passive aggressive behavior, and let ruminating thoughts take over, you are only creating more stress for yourself:

- You are not solving the problem, you are just hiding from having to deal with it
- This behavior may be very frustrating for others around you
- Your problems are growing because you are not in the driver's seat.

Here is how you can get in the driver's seat within two seconds

Ask yourself this: How much do I want to get in the driver's seat of my life right now? Get out of your own head and give yourself a number. Then take a quick action and get up. It's that simple.

As you are getting out of your own head and giving yourself a number, take a small action that would symbolize this, like standing up, banging your hand on a table, or putting your hand on your heart. Any action that symbolizes power for you.

You just broke the cycle.

If you are reverting back to ruminating thoughts or repeating the same behaviors (you are procrastinating or being passive aggressive) do it again:

How much do I want to get in the driver's seat of my life right now?

Get out of your own head and give yourself a number.

Then take a quick action and get up.

The secret is to snap out of a cycle. The only way to do that is by repeating a mantra that communicates getting in the driver's seat of your life and reclaiming control, and then taking a small action that symbolizes that.

That's it. You are out of the cycle. Now to keep you out of there, let's move on to step 2.

Step 2: Get crystal clear on what matters to you the most (your 10s)

You have a shield that can keep you safer and healthier, both physically and mentally. That shield works for everyone, but it works exceptionally well for people who are sensitive, prone to anxiety, or are going through a tough time.

That shield is available to you as well, and it will make you significantly stronger. That shield is incredibly strong and its strength is backed up by science.

Your shield is called **purpose**.

Here is some data for you to consider. I have compiled it from recent research.

Longevity

- Purpose is correlated with a lifespan up to 7 years longer than average (Journal of Psychosomatic Medicine, 2008)
- Purpose is correlated with a reduction in mortality rates for people over 50 years old (University of Michigan, 2019)
- Purpose is correlated with a reduction in the likelihood of stroke by 50% (Rush University, 2016)
- Purpose is correlated with a reduction in the likelihood of death by coronary heart disease by 23% (Mt. Sinai, 2015)
- Purpose is correlated with a reduction in the likelihood of death from stroke by 72% (Koizumi, 2008)

Sleep

- Purpose is correlated with better sleep (Kim, 2015)

Mental Health and Well-being

- Purpose is correlated with higher levels of contentment by 42% (Leider/Metlife, 2009)
- Purpose is correlated with more progressed identity formation (Florida International University, 2014)
- Purpose is correlated with greater levels of self-esteem (University of Rochester, 2010)

- Purpose is correlated with higher levels of grit (Carleton University, 2014)
- Purpose is correlated with greater ease in making healthy choices (University of Pennsylvania, 2019)
- Purpose is correlated with increased life satisfaction (Journal of Happiness Studies, 2016)
- Purpose is correlated with an increase in resilience to resistance, obstacles and strain (APA, 2009)
- Purpose is correlated with a decrease in repetitive negative thoughts and associated stress (University of Groningen, 2019)
- Purpose is correlated with a decrease in the incidence of depression in adults (Journal of Clinical Psychology, 1980, University of Manchester, 2010)
- Purpose is correlated with higher levels of hope (Cornell, 2009)
- Purpose is correlated with a decrease in incidents of depression in teens (PNAS, 2014)
- Purpose is correlated with lower levels of burnout, trauma and stress in the lives of social service workers (University of Nevada Reno, 2019)

Emotional Regulation

- Purpose is correlated with improved impulse control (Cornell, 2016, University of Michigan and Ohio State University, 2012)
- Purpose is correlated with greater levels of relaxation (University of Texas Austin, 2006)
- Purpose is correlated with a reduction in fear and anxiety responses (University of Toronto, 2015)
- Purpose is correlated with better emotional recovery (University of Wisconsin Madison, 2007)
- Purpose is correlated with an increased ability to cope with pain (University of New Mexico Albuquerque, 2009)
- Purpose is correlated with an increase in coping with adversity (Stanford, 2019)

Learning, Memory and Cognition

- Purpose is correlated with a doubling of the likelihood of learning something new each day (Gallup/Healthways, 2013)
- Purpose increases academic tenacity (Gates Foundation, 2014)
- Purpose increases lifelong learning and achievement (UNESCO, 2015)
- Purpose is correlated with higher scores for memory, executive function and overall cognition (Aging, Neuropsychology and Cognition, 2016)
- Purpose enhances "cognitive reserve," the biological strength and resilience of brain cells to injury and degradation (Cerebrum, 2015)
- Purpose is correlated with faster brain processing speed, more accurate memory, and lower levels of disability and depression in aging adults (Windsor, Curtis and Luszsz, Flinders University, Developmental Psychology, July 2015)
- Purpose protects against cognitive decline in older adults (Chung-Ang University, 2019)

Relationships and Love

- Purpose is correlated with stronger and more abundant social ties (University College London, 2019)
- Purpose is correlated with higher levels of sexual enjoyment (University of Pittsburgh, 2011)
- Purpose is correlated with increased levels of attraction (Social, Psychological and Personality Science, 2010)
- Purpose is correlated with a 31% increase in the feeling of being in love (Leider/Metlife, 2009)

Addiction, Trauma and Recovery

- Purpose is correlated with a 50% reduction in six-month cocaine relapse rates (Brown University, 2011)

- Purpose is correlated with lower incidence of Internet Gaming Disorder (University of Macau, 2019)
- Purpose is correlated with decreased PTSD symptoms (Indiana-Purdue University, 2020)

Purpose is not something big or vague. Sometimes it is as simple and as powerful as your family, health, or financial stability. Life is not that complicated. Sometimes the most simple things are the most meaningful things in our lives.

It's hard sometimes to just stop and think what those things are for you. But when you actually think about it: can anything be more important?

Forget all the noise. Forget your friends and what they do. Forget what your parents think. Forget expectations and social media and the things that annoy you and bother you.

What matters the most to you? Take a piece of paper and a pen and write it down. Then get out of your own head and write a number for yourself. How much does this thing that you just wrote down matter to you?

Is it 1?
Is it 2?
Is it 3?
Is it 4?
Is it 5?
Is it 6?
Is it 7?
Is it 8?
Is it 9?
Is it 10?

Whatever you wrote there on that piece of paper is your shield and compass. It will show you the way to go, and it will protect you when you feel scared or confused. This is your lighthouse and it will help you navigate your life with all challenges and in stormy water.

> To Combat Anxiety and Being Overwhelmed:
>
> Step 1: Get in the driver's seat and take action to manage your stress.
>
> Step 2: Get crystal clear on what matters to you the most (Your 10s). Step 3: Purpose = resilience.

Getting in the driver's seat means that from now on you manage your life, not your anxiety. Your anxiety may still be there, at least for a while, but it is going to sit in the backseat of your life. It will not navigate anymore. This is how you take control:

GETTING IN THE DRIVER'S SEAT AND TAKING ACTION

Anxious thoughts

Take action to feel better

Get clear on your 10s, direction, resilience

Sense of control

Get in the driver's seat and take control no matter what

It may happen that getting in the driver's seat of your life will seem odd to others. You owe no explanation to no one. The only thing that matters is that you are in control, not your fears.

I remember when my dad was dying from cancer. My mom got cancer at the same time, and the same type too. She ended up recovering but my dad was in his last days. It was so sad to say goodbye to this great man, who was such a caretaker we all joked the only reason he didn't breastfeed is that he couldn't technically do it. I was very attached to him, and profoundly overwhelmed by having both of my parents so sick at the same time. On the outside I was holding it together, but the stress was accumulating on the inside. Then one day I came home and my daughter was looking for her soccer clothes in the dryer, leaving clean laundry all over the floor. There was a complete discrepancy between what she did (a minor infraction only) and my response—a complete meltdown, crying for hours, angry at everyone around me, my day destroyed.

Was it my fault that I got overwhelmed? Not at all.

Was this a logical response? Not from a parental standpoint, for sure. But from my own perspective, yes. I was anxious and sad, and if this hadn't been the last straw for me, something else would have been. I was on the edge of a breakdown, and this happened to be the tipping point.

After crying for hours, I called my husband who was on a business trip. I told him I had just had a huge meltdown, that I was a mess, and that I needed to get to the finish line not only for my parents but for all of us. And that I knew it sounded crazy, but I needed to go on vacation for a few days and pull myself together without my parents knowing.

It sounds a bit odd, right? To go on vacation at a time like this. But I did. And it was a good decision for sure. There was some drama toward the end—my dad in his last days tried to commit suicide and was saved at the last minute, just to have a few more months with us and many precious moments before he left us for good.

The action I took may seem questionable for some. That doesn't matter. I want you to think of what would've happened if I didn't take action. How much worse the entire situation would've been.

Remember this: Anxiety and being overwhelmed = a cycle of feeling debilitated, powerless, focused on worry, and stymied into a lack of action.

Well, here is the opposite of all of that. Action.

There is someone who can pull you out of that cycle. And that someone knows you better than anyone else.

That someone is you.

Don't apologize to anyone. You know what is right for you. Do it. Take action now.

DON'T ASK: CAN I?

INSTEAD ASK: WHAT DECISIONS DO I NEED TO MAKE TO MAKE IT HAPPEN?

PART 4

GET IN THE DRIVER'S SEAT OF YOUR WORK AND CAREER

CHAPTER THIRTEEN

HOW TO BE THE LEADER YOU ARE MEANT TO BE

"Don't follow the crowd. Let the crowd follow you." –Margaret Thatcher

This part of the book is going to focus on leadership. After many years of working with corporate leaders around the world, there is one thing I need you to know. Leadership never happens just in the workplace. Leadership is not about a title. **Leadership is about becoming.** It is about becoming accountable, becoming decisive, becoming empathetic and becoming confident. It is about becoming a source of motivation and a role model to people around you. And above all, it is about taking charge. It is about getting in the driver's seat, navigating your destiny, and acting rather than reacting, no matter what is on your plate. I have seen amazing leadership from people in their homes. I have witnessed remarkable leadership of others withing their communities, and I have met and worked with some outstanding leaders in the workplace. The common thing with all of them is becoming that person who takes charge and gets in the driver's seat.

I have gone through that shift myself. I have learned to get in the driver's seat and take charge. I wasn't always like that. I learned to take charge and get in the driver's seat of my life and destiny. And I now know this for sure—I cannot control life's events, but I can take charge of my choices. That made me the leader I am today. And it changed my life.

Here are the key aspects of leadership I want you to get in the driver's seat of. All of these combined will make you the leader you are meant to be.

> "The greatest leader is not necessarily the one who does the greatest things. It is the one that gets the people to do the greatest things" –Ronald Reagan

How to become the most accountable leader you know?

Accountable leaders take full responsibility for their decisions. This is why, no matter what leadership position you are in within your company, community or family, everything boils down to getting maximum clarity on what you are deciding, and then standing behind those decisions no matter what.

If I was to summarize the basis of all accountability for leaders in one word it would be this: clarity. Too often I encounter leaders who are unclear themselves, give unclear instructions, and lead confused and overwhelmed teams. When you become clear on what you decide, you know what you want and you know that you stand behind it 100%. As an **accountable leader** you provide clarity on what I call WHW:

- **W**hat you want
- **H**ow the team can achieve what you want
- **W**hat is in it for everyone (potential gains on individual and team levels)

As an example, lets apply this both at home with your family and at work with your team. You'll see that the same principles apply. This is great because when you discover things that work, you can apply them in every aspect of your life, both at work and home, and enjoy the benefits in all fronts of your life.

At home:

- **W**hat you want: more help around the house
- **H**ow the team (the family) can achieve what you want: follow daily list of chores that delegate work to everybody
- **W**hat in it for everyone: together we can have a fed dog, a clean kitchen, and happy parents who are not stressed out (sounds like a pretty big gain to me)

At work:

- **W**hat you want: project done by Monday for the client
- **H**ow the team can achieve what you want: clear guidelines for the team for step-by-step project completion, and who is responsible for what and by when
- **W**hat is in it for everyone (potential gains on individual and team levels): client retains your services, potential bonus, praise and recognition from leader to team, team is winning at target goals.

2 Second Decisions make you the most accountable leader you know, because you gain the clarity you need. You know what you want, and you know that you are honing in on your 9s an 10s. You stand behind them with confidence, and communicate clearly with your team what matters the most and what you want from them.

When you are striving to become the most accountable leader you know, you need to know what you are up against:

Accountability  **Blame, Excuses**

Blaming others when there is a problem, or finding explanations or excuses, is a human tendency. In fact, psychologists have long concluded that people tend to judge others more harshly for their negative actions, assigning fault and blame more often than praise or responsibility. The reason for this is simple. The brain takes a lot of energy from our body (about 20%) and is not really interested in spending more energy than it is already doing. Think about it: blaming others or making excuses is an easy solution that does not require much energy from the brain, so it defaults to that. Accountability is much more work. You have to figure out your responsibility for the situation, you have to clarify it with yourself, then you have to decide what to change and act accordingly. This is a lot of work for the brain, so it tends to default to the easy solution: let's just blame someone else and be done with it.

I want you to use 2 Second Decisions to curb your brain's tendency to enact quick fixes by finding excuses and blaming others. Take these three steps:

Step 1: Declare

Declare to yourself in one sentence what the problem is. Write it down. This way you ensure clarity for yourself first.

Step 2: Define

Get out of your own head and define how much of this is your responsibility.

Is it 1?
Is it 2?

Is it 3?

Is it 4?

Is it 5?

Is it 6?

Is it 7?

Is it 8?

Is it 9?

Is it 10?

Step 3: Decide

Decide to change something on your end in order to hold yourself accountable to a solution. This could be:

- Delegate better (define how)
- Assign different responsibilities to different people
- Become clearer in your directions (define how)
- Communicate better (specify how)
- And more

Now act with confidence. Change will not come from blaming others or finding reasons why something happened. Change will only come from you taking accountability and deciding to do something differently in order to get different results.

How to become the most decisive leader you know

Decisiveness is one of the most important qualities of leaders in every position and industry, but only a few leaders understand their decision-making process and how to become more decisive. It is hard to understand why these incredibly important skills are still rare enough to distinguish between great leaders and average managers.

Have you ever worked with a leader who couldn't make up their mind—who was constantly asking others what they thought but never come to any conclusions themselves? if you have experienced this you know how confusing, anxiety-provoking and frustrating an indecisive leader can be.

> "The great leaders of the world were men and women of quick decision." –Napoleon Hill

Let's look at the 6 pillars of decisive leaders. You are going to demonstrate all of these by mastering the power of 2 Second Decisions.

You will become more credible:

Decisive leaders do what they say they will do. They are responsible and accountable. Once you use 2 Second Decisions you will be clear in your decisions, and can quickly and effectively hold yourself accountable to your own decisions. This clarity and following up will make you more credible, and will instill confidence in your team in terms of your decisions, strategy, instructions and actions.

You will become more confident:

Decisive leaders know what they want with clarity and confidence. This makes it hard for others to second-guess their decisions, and it builds more trust. The confidence you are gaining by making 2 Second Decisions is a loop that will work in your favor in the most powerful way.

THE 2 SECOND DECISIONS CONFIDENCE LOOP

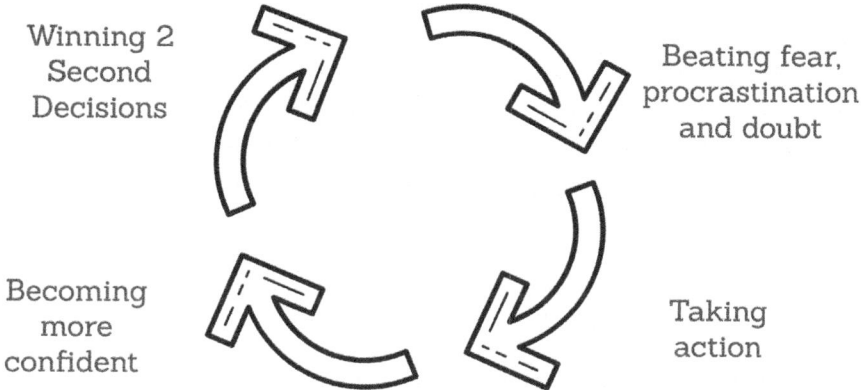

Winning 2 Second Decisions

Beating fear, procrastination and doubt

Becoming more confident

Taking action

You will be quick to decide:

Decisive leaders decide with speed and clarity. In order to shine as the best leader you are, I want you to get out of your own head, use the intelligence you have, and trust yourself, your experience and your intuition. Delaying your decision will lead to hesitation, analysis paralysis and fear. Move forward with confidence and make winning decisions fast. This will allow you to carry out strategies, adapt quickly, and provide value and support to both your team members and your customers.

You will become more trusted:

It's human nature to trust decisive leaders and follow them, because it instils in people a sense of confidence. Leaders who demonstrate confidence are trusted more by others. This is because of a mind bias people have called the confidence heuristic. This basically means that people assume if someone is confident, they know what they are saying, and they don't check so much into the details. In other words, as a leader, keep in mind that confidence comes before details, because if you have lost people's trust, the details will not matter at that point. Once you become more trusted, you will have to spend less time and energy on the nay-sayers. Your own confidence will address their anxiety and doubt.

You will become more bold:

Indecision itself is the root of much fear, stress and worry. Making powerful decisions means you are at a point of overcoming your fears. Today, more than ever, learning how to make decisions in the face of uncertainty makes all the difference.

You will become more Intuitive:

One of the most important attributes you will have as a great leader is your ability to make tough decisions by learning to trust your intuitive instincts. Bill Gates says, "Often you have to rely on intuition." This means that while keeping all facts in mind, at the end of the day you need to get out of your own head and give it a number, also based on what you feel in your gut.

> A great leader navigates to find simple solutions to the most complicated problems. Always strive to simplify what seems to be complex.

How to become a great leader by showing empathy

The ability to empathize with your team is one of the most powerful skills any leader can have. While many leaders fail to work on their soft skills and focus on strategy, vision and execution, businesses and corporations are at the end of the day about people. For that reason, empathy plays an incredibly critical role in your success as a leader.

Empathy is about being a person before anything else you are or do. It comes before your title and before any responsibilities you have. In other words, on your scale of 0 to 10, it should be up there in your 9s and 10s.

Empathy means being able to understand the needs of others. It means you're aware of their feelings and thinking.

Now, let's get this straight. This is not a touchy-feely skill. It is difficult to master and demanding to maintain, and it has a major impact on your success as a leader.

You see, your leadership is ultimately about others. Being the greatest leader you can be means you constantly expand your ability to inspire the people you lead to take actions beyond what they thought was possible, and that you lead them toward a vision and execution that is compelling and inspiring.

Empathy is the foundation of those actions. In order to motivate people to do all those things, you need to get out of the mindset of judging them and into the mindset of trying to understand where they are coming from, and moving them into action exactly from where they are at.

Here are four ways you can use 2 Second Decisions immediately, to become a great leader by showing more empathy.

1. Use 2 Second Decisions to Become a better listener.

One of the easiest ways for you to improve your empathy skills is to become a better listener. Remember this: every conversation you have is an opportunity to not only practice listening, but also to observe and absorb information the other person is communicating to you.

Many people don't know how to truly listen. Listening is simple but requires your focus. Pay attention, don't interrupt, don't pay attention to distractions, and just be there for the other person and give them your undivided attention.

Just by the simple act of listening, you are communicating to the other person that they matter to you. Ask yourself this: how important is it for me to truly listen to this person right now? If you rate it high, be there, listen and give that person your undivided attention. Communicate to them that you care and that you are listening, both verbally (showing them in words that you are hearing and understanding them) and non-verbally (eye contact, nodding, body language).

2. Use 2 Second Decisions to build rapport with your team.

Empathy is not only about being able to read and understand what the other person is going through, but also communicating to them that you are getting them and that you are with them.

Use 2 Second Decisions to stop yourself from judging people, and instead open your mind to what you do not know about them. To every communication, there are three layers:

1. The layer of what is being communicated to you, verbally and non-verbally
2. The layer of what you don't know
3. The layer of what you may be assuming

Dealing with the layer of what is being communicated to you is the easiest part. All you need to do is be present and listen.

Dealing with what you don't know is harder. How can you be empathetic to things you don't even know about? You can be empathetic to what you don't know simply by recognizing there is a lot you don't know about the other person, and giving them the benefit of a doubt. Always ask yourself: on a scale of 0 to 10, am I giving that person the benefit of a doubt? This will serve as a reminder to give people the benefit of a doubt, because this is what empathetic leadership is all about. This doesn't mean that people in your team can do whatever they want. It means that you lead them by being fully aware there is more to every situation than you know, and that your job is to help that person thrive regardless of their circumstances, not to judge them.

The layer of dealing with what you may be assuming is both the most challenging one and the most rewarding one. Remember that your mind plays tricks on you in how you perceive yourself and others within the reality of your life. I want you to use 2 Second Decisions in order to stop yourself from assuming. Always ask yourself: on a scale of 0 to 10, how sure am I that this is not just something that I am assuming?

3. Use 2 Second Decisions to be authentic.

Empathy can't be faked. If you don't really connect with your people and you don't truly care about what they are going through, it will be very apparent to them. The only way you can truly win their trust is to be authentic.

I am a great believer in transparency and honesty. You can't expect others to be genuine with you if you are not genuine with them. There is something in being genuine that transcends words or actions. People feel when you are real, and they feel when you are fake. Too often I hear leaders responding to team members in a way that sounds forced, almost mechanical. Saying what they think is right is a format that seems right, but the outcome is neither sincere nor empathetic. It actually has the opposite impact—it creates a distance and lack of trust.

Leaders don't need to hide their emotions. If you're happy, show it. If you're angry, show it. Being honest is the ultimate form of respect to the other person. It makes you relatable and approachable.

Use 2 Second Decisions to ask yourself: on a scale of 0 to 10, am I being honest and open right now? If you got out of your own head and gave yourself a low number, ask yourself this: how can I connect better?

4. Use 2 Second Decisions to ask questions.

The best way to understand how someone is feeling is to simply ask them.

Believe it or not, many leaders overlook this option. Leaders who do not ask questions end up making assumptions, instead of discovering what would really help people and make cultural improvements.

Get out of your own head and mind biases, and just ask.

> "The word why not only taught me to ask, but also to think." –Anne Frank

Here are three types of questions you can choose from, based on the situation, your gut feeling, and what you think may work best.

1. **Direct questions**
   The goal: direct information. Simply ask what is on your mind. Make eye contact; be direct, honest and respectful; and just ask. Honest questions get honest answers. Sometimes that is all you need.

2. **Circular questions**

   The goal: indirect information. Circular questions are questions about other people as a means of gaining information. I usually use these questions with people who have a hard time opening up (this is great with teenagers and people who do not trust you yet). Ask people about other people, how they are doing and what is going on. This way the person does not feel threatened, and discusses other team members or situations while indirectly also discussing themselves and gradually opening up.

3. **Scaling questions**

   The goal: bottom-line answer. Scaling questions help you gather information quickly. In scaling questions you ask the other person to scale from 0 to 10 their answer to a question you have. The benefit: this allows you to gain clarity within two seconds.

Remember, empathy is about being a person. Leadership is about being a person. Just be a person. It is the foundation of all success.

WHEN YOU TAKE THE TIME TO ASK ME A QUESTION, YOU SHOW ME YOU CARE ABOUT ME AND THAT YOU ARE ON MY TEAM.

NOTHING CREATES MORE ENGAGEMENT THAN THAT.

CHAPTER FOURTEEN
EMPOWER AND INSPIRE

"As we look ahead into the next century, leaders will be those who empower others." –Bill Gates

A lot of the seemingly complex challenges you are facing as a leader, and with other people in your life in general, can be solved by strategically using empowerment. It's a simple tool you are already aware of, that you already know how to use, but that you constantly underestimate. I often ask groups of leaders that I talk to: give me an example of five people you have empowered this past week. What I usually get is a room full of leaders scratching their heads trying to remember who in their team they have whole heartedly complimented this past week.

As people, we tend to underestimate the power that empowerment has on other people and use it much less than we should. We do not use it enough with our kids, spouses, family members, team members and clients.

Old-style leadership, as much as old-style parenting, was about telling the other person what to do. Leadership used to be all about command and control, being as authoritative as possible. The leader was supposed to have all the power and answers, and employees were expected to do as they were told and follow the rules. Not that following the rules is not expected today, but today's market is a lot more innovation-based, and companies build heavily on resourcefulness and out-of-the-box thinking. All that innovation and resourcefulness cannot come just from the leader, and so a bigger place is created for a team of empowered, capable and innovative individuals who together come up with the most innovative and brilliant ideas.

> Leadership has shifted from being the best to empowering team members to be their best.

Empowering someone is about making them feel you believe in them, trust them and think they are capable and reliable. As people, we all want to feel good about ourselves.

In spite of the fact that research shows consistently that feeling good about yourself makes you much more productive, many leaders do not utilize empowerment as the great motivational tool it is.

> Most people don't have someone who truly believes in them. Be that someone.

Look at everyone around you, at work, at home and everywhere else in your life. Everyone around you is addicted to a certain chemical. When they don't get enough of that chemical, they get frustrated, angry, anxious, and difficult to deal with. The chemical I am referring to fades quickly.

That chemical is dopamine.

Dopamine is a type of neurotransmitter. Your body makes it and your nervous system uses it in order to send messages between different nerve cells, sort of like a chemical messenger in your body. Dopamine is a major player in feeling pleasure, and helps you and everyone around you focus and find things interesting and motivating. People who do not have enough dopamine released in their bodies feel depressed, sad and anxious.

Now here is the mind hack. Every time you praise or empower someone, dopamine is released in their brain. This creates feelings of pride and pleasure. When you and other people around you experience pleasure, you want more. We are all pleasure-seeking creatures.

Now here is an interesting fact. The dopamine release people experience when they are recognized and empowered doesn't last very long. It is something you need to repeat daily or at least no longer than weekly, in order to create what we call the reward-repeat loop—your employee does something great, you empower them by recognizing it, dopamine is released, and they keep doing something else in a great way, expecting to feel dopamine released in their body again because you recognize them. If you fail to recognize them, you are breaking the reward-repeat loop, and by that working against your own interests. By neglecting to recognize, simply because you were busy or distracted or didn't think enough to say anything, you are demotivating a valuable team member and hurting not only their success but also the team's as well as yours.

We are all addicted to dopamine to some extent. The question is how you utilize that as a leader. If you know how to recognize, empower and appreciate, then everybody wins: the employee, the team, the organization and you. And the best part of all? It doesn't cost anything to anyone, besides your focus for just a few minutes. Small price to pay.

An "employee recognition day" once a year does not do the work. Those are good to have but they are simply not enough. Appreciation, gratitude and empowerment should happen on a daily basis, as part of your second nature and as part of your day-to-day interactions with other people.

THE MOTIVATION FORMULA

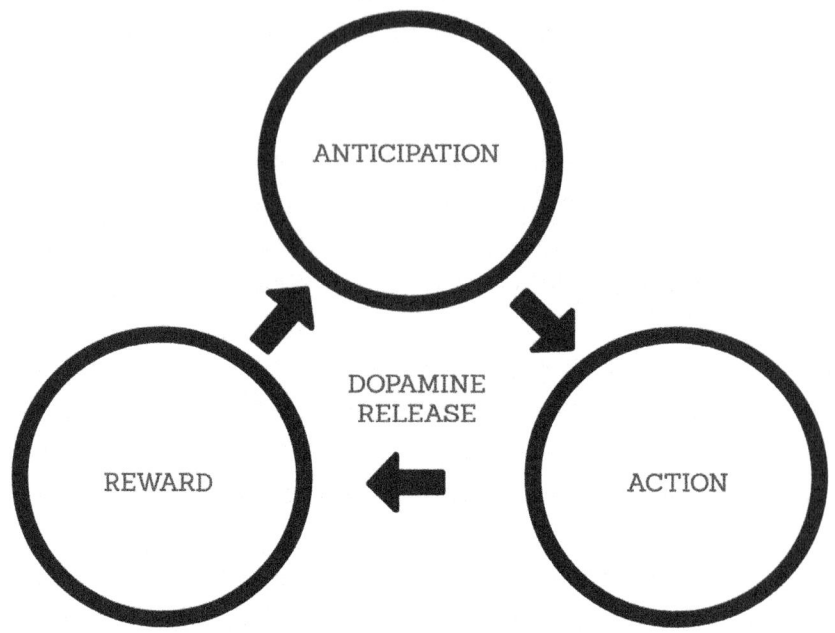

Think about the negativity bias that we spoke about earlier. I want you to keep this bias in mind every day, because it impacts your tendency to empower people around you a lot less than you should. The mind always focuses on the negative: what employees messed up on, what balls they dropped, what they could have done better. At home your mind causes you to focus on behaviors your kid needs to work on. The good efforts you tend to take for granted are what you need to focus on. Those things hold the potential for dopamine release and the opportunity for a reward-repeat loop.

Imagine yourself standing in a dark area holding a big flashlight. You can choose to shed the light on good things people are doing, recognizing how capable they are and believing in them, or you can choose to focus on their mess-ups and mistakes. Be the person who believes in someone. Be the person who empowers them. Who sees them. A lot of people only see themselves.

> "Outstanding leaders go out of their way to boost the self-esteem of their personnel. If people believe in themselves, it's amazing what they can accomplish" –Sam Walton

Your personal *perception* of reality is determined by the beliefs you hold. This does not necessarily make them real, except for the fact that you believe they are. Your beliefs create and dictate what your attitudes are.

Most of your choices throughout your life were *programmed* very early in life by parents, peers, teachers, and other role models. As a child, you internalized their core beliefs as facts.

I want you to stop and think about that for a minute. Who are the adults who shaped the way you perceive yourself?

Did they believe in you?

Did they not believe in you?

How did that impact the way you perceived yourself?

How did that impact your perception of what you can and cannot do?

How did that impact your life?

You are surrounded by people who doubt themselves. Who no one believed in, or believed in enough. The greatest privilege and moral responsibility every leader has is to lift others to believe they can stretch their limits and do amazing things.

Think of your role as a leader as a coach. Can a coach produce a successful player if they do not believe in them? Can a coach produce a winning player if they do not empower then build on their strengths?

> "A good coach can change a game. A great coach can change a life." –John Wooden

Use 2 Second Decisions to check yourself every day. Ask yourself, on a scale of 0 to 10, how much did I empower this person in the last seven days? If you scored low, get to work. Here are 7 "empowerment hacks" you can use to motivate the people around you every day.

Remember: empowerment works for low morale, low engagement, uncertainty, and when people are coping with challenges in their personal or professional lives. Use it. As long as you are genuine, it will work.

"I trust you!"

Instead of micromanaging someone, which is the ultimate demonstration of lack of trust, tell someone you trust them and then actually trust them. This does not mean you leave them without guidance, but it means you guide them by giving them the information they need in order to succeed. If you are micromanaging someone, it comes from your own anxieties. Work on managing your own anxieties and give the other person the tools, space and trust they need in order to succeed.

"This is what I need!"

Communicate clearly. It is your job as a leader to communicate with a kind of clarity that primes the other person for success. Too many leaders do not invest the time needed for clear communication because they doubt what they ask for will actually be done the way they expect. Let me put it this way: I want you to communicate so clearly that there will be zero chance not to understand what needs to happen in order for that person to succeed.

"Let's talk!"

One-on-one conversations matter. They matter at work with your employees and they matter at home with your kids. Find a quiet space. Create uninterrupted time. Take the time to highlight good things you didn't have a chance to talk about.

If you are talking to your employee, ask them about their family. Make sure you remember important information. Show them you care. By taking the time to care, and making the time to talk, you are communicating to the other person non-verbally how much they matter to you.

"Take a training!"

Make sure to communicate to the other person the greatness that you see in them. Alongside that, make sure to identify opportunities for their growth. Highlight courses, work with them if they go after a certain degree, support any learning. Highlight the potential contribution to the organization. A team member who becomes more has more to give. Can anything be more powerful?

"Got an idea? I'd love to hear it!"

Too often I hear of companies where employees don't feel comfortable to share innovative ideas because they are afraid of being criticized by others. Create a culture where everyone can feel empowered to think, express and share their input. If someone comes forward with input that doesn't sit right with you, don't be quick to crush them. Give them the space to express their input. Maybe this time their input is irrelevant, but you don't want to miss their next input because it may be amazing.

"I love what you did with that proposal!"

When you recognize something good, be specific. "Great job" means very little. It is a specific explanation of what you liked that does the work.

When you recognize effort, show that you care not only in your words but also in your body language and tone of voice.

Most importantly, be genuine. Do not acknowledge someone when you don't really see the point. It doesn't have any impact if it is not genuine. People see through it right away.

"If anyone can do it, it's you!"

Challenge your team members to exceed their limits, and tell them you believe in them and that they can do it. If you keep them within their comfort zone, what's the point of empowerment if the effort is little?

Check in with yourself within 2 seconds: on a scale of 0 to 10, how much did I empower that person in the last seven days? If you scored low, get to work on doing better!

ASK YOURSELF THIS ONE
QUESTION EVERYDAY:

DID I EMPOWER PEOPLE
AROUND ME TODAY, OR DID I
MAKE THEM FEEL SMALL?

CHAPTER FIFTEEN

SPEAK UP AND BE HEARD

"Speak your mind, even if your voice shakes." –Maggie Kuhn

When I was in 5ᵗʰ grade, the whole class decided to single out this one girl and not talk to her. Her name was Sharon. The reason was silly, something about a boy. They all followed the leader, another girl who totally set the tone for everyone back then. The more daring girls said they were 'neutral,' as if not taking a stand actually meant being 'nice.' I remember finding the whole thing to be stupid and unfair, and declared that I supported the girl, Sharon. I wasn't afraid and I wasn't bothered by speaking my mind. I didn't even care if the whole class singled me out too, and most of all I refused to be 'neutral.'

In retrospect I kind of feel proud of that moment, but back then I was just a fifth-grade girl who took a stand. Sharon and I became best friends and our friendship lasted many, many years. I remember being surprised how little opposition I had when I took a stand and spoke my mind. I really think they were too confused by the fact that I just didn't follow the rules (in retrospect, such a typical Michelle move). Soon enough, after I made sure the class knew that I was taking a stand with Sharon and against all of them, they backed off and started talking to her again. I remember how long it took her to forgive the bystanders, the 'neutral' girls. Those were the girls who were actually friends with her before this whole 'not talking to Sharon' class crisis started. She resented them more than the instigators. I learned this in fifth grade for sure: there is no such thing as being 'neutral,' and bystanders are the worst.

But for every time I've spoken up, I have another time I didn't. Many years later I had my first speaking engagement, at a conference in Canada for elementary school teachers. When I got to the conference, the organizer pointed at a podium and said, "Michelle, I just need you to stand there." I was so confused. How can I be engaging if I just stand behind the podium the whole time? Hesitant, I asked him, "Are you sure? I would rather move around and interact with people." The guy just looked at me impatiently and said, "Michelle, please. I just need you to stand there behind the podium and please don't move from there. It's very important."

I wanted to say something but I wasn't really sure what to say. The whole situation was quite overwhelming, and even though I knew deep inside that this was a really bad idea, I said nothing. I did what he asked and stayed behind the podium the whole time, and somehow I got through it. If you've ever been at one of my talks you'll know I move around a lot. It's just how I do it. That day I wanted to move, talk to the audience and do my thing, but I couldn't. That day I wasn't me. I was just this very limited person behind a podium with very few options for what she could do. When I watched my video of the presentation, I was so mad at myself. Why didn't I speak up? Why did I just comply? I promised myself to never do that again. To lead and not to follow. To set the rules rather than let them set me. I've never stood behind a podium for an entire presentation ever again.

Life is short. Take a stand. If you've got something to say—say it.

So what happened to that brave girl from 5th grade? Why did I not speak up? And where in your life do you find yourself wondering the same thing? Where in your life do you feel you should have spoken up, that you should have made your opinion heard, and you didn't?

Let's look together at what we are actually dealing with when we don't take a stand and don't speak our mind.

We are dealing with fear of rejection.

When I started researching the issue of rejection I found that people fear rejection all the time, in every human interaction. Did you know that in your brain, the same neural pathways are activated when you are rejected as when you experience physical pain? Now you know why rejection hurts so much. It actually physically hurts.

Historically, back to your human ancestors, being accepted by the tribe was a matter of survival. Rejection by the tribe was a serious and imminent threat to survival.

It is not rejection you are battling when you decide if you should speak your mind or not. Rejection may happen or not; that is not something you have control over. After all, in my 5th grade story, rejection didn't happen.

It is not about rejection. It is about the fear of rejection. What you are up against is fear.

The sting of rejection can really pierce the heart. It is extremely hard not to take rejection personally. And yet the success of every leader comes from being innovative and bold, putting fears aside and taking a stand. <u>You become a true leader when you take rejection into consideration, and you still speak up and take a stand. That is what true leadership is all about.</u>

> "Trying to get everyone to like you is a sign of mediocracy." –Oren Harari

I'd like to introduce a new mindset to you. A new idea. It is very simple: not everybody has to like you.

Shocking, I know.

But your road to becoming the leader you are meant to be is centered around exactly that—letting go of the idea that you need to be approved of and liked. And from that place, speaking up and being heard, not caring what other people say.

This concept of not letting go of the need to be liked is very liberating. Having a constant need to be liked by everyone, especially when you are in a leadership position, is an exhausting way to go about life.

Here is the cycle that you are currently at:

You fear being
rejected

You lose
power

You avoid
speaking
out

The first thing you need to know is that the fear of rejection is an irrational fear, one that has you convinced that people will not accept you or approve of you if you say something they do not approve of. This is a debilitating fear that has incredible impact on your choices, decisions and actions. It causes you to do things that you normally wouldn't do. It has impact on your career, your relationships and your everyday decisions.

Instead, try the following. Look for the next opportunity you have to speak up. This can be a team meeting or a meeting with your boss. You can also practice this outside of work with a family member or friend you tend to comply with instead of speaking your mind.

Combating your fear of rejection is detrimental to your success in every possible aspect of your life. Here is how it is hurting you:

It prevents you from saying what you think

You fear rejection and for that reason hold back on expressing your opinions on certain things, because you fear that people will reject them, ridicule you for them, or not accept you because of them. This can become so debilitating that you literally don't do anything that contradicts another person's opinion. Instead of you being in the driver's seat, speaking your mind and making an impact, your fear of being rejected is in the driver's seat, and causes you to say and do whatever you need to in order to prevent the pain of a potential rejection.

It causes you to copy other people's behavior

The fear of rejection has such a strong impact on you that you are afraid to be different, unique and original. You are afraid to be yourself. So you talk like others do, you dress like others do, and you act like others do. You are so driven by your fear that you copy someone else who is not really you. The fear of being rejected by others causes you to lose touch with who you are.

Instead of having an internal locus of control, you have an external one

Locus of control means how much you feel you are in control of your life. Because you are controlled by your fear of rejection, you have an external locus of control, which means that the people around you are the ones who control your mood and state of mind, not you.

You become too needy

Rejection has such a strong impact on you that you are afraid to be rejected to the point that this becomes a motivating force for your actions. In your subconscious, you are constantly asking yourself: what do I need to say or do, just so that I am not rejected right now? You rely on other people not to reject you means you depend on them and their approval in order to feel secure and strong. The fact that you feel you need those other people in order to feel happy is making you needy.

You are easily manipulated

Other people around you notice how much you need their approval and sense your weakness. Soon enough, they start manipulating you and not appreciating you. You see, people value other people who are confident, who dare to be unique, and who dare to speak their mind.

> "You were never Little Red Riding Hood. You were always the wolf." –Abby Wombach

Let's talk about where this fear of rejection comes from, because it's time for you to let it go and empower yourself to be true to who you are and speak your mind. Let's look at these two main possible reasons for why you are not speaking up and being heard, and how you can combat each of them.

Possible reason #1: You have poor self-esteem

Check yourself: do you have an external locus of control? Do you feel that others know better than you? That others are better than you? A few things could have caused that:

- Messages you got in childhood from adults about yourself in comparison to others
- Perfectionism
- Living with a parent or life partner who always criticizes you
- Past experiences of failure
- Past experiences of rejection
- Past traumas

I want you to remember this:

Feeling like you have no accomplishments  Lack of self-confidence

THEREFORE:

Creating any wins, even small ones  More self-confidence

More self-confidence  Speaking up and gaining even more wins!

Telling you that you need to speak up will not create the change here. What will create the change is creating wins, even small ones, and feeling good about yourself as a result. I want you to start using 2 Second Decisions every day to get in the driver's seat, take charge of your time, take charge of your goals, and take charge of what matters to you the most. Win by win, you'll start adding more and more success under your belt, and before you know it you'll have a lot to say. And guess what—a lot of people will listen. Mark my words.

Possible reason #2: You have poor social skills

Considering how confident and outspoken I am today, it is hard to believe how incredibly poor my social skills were for the first 25 years of my life. I really picked up most of my social skills from my husband. When we started dating and he'd take me to meet his friends, I would sit there in silence and not say a word. Of course I had things I wanted to say, but I felt too timid and awkward. By now I have known some of these people for 25 years or more, and I feel very comfortable about speaking up and saying anything I want, but back then I didn't. I had poor social skills, I felt awkward around other people, I kept to myself, and only felt comfortable with the two friends I had. I was afraid of— guess what—being rejected. I didn't think I was funny, I had no clue what to say, and it felt safest to just not say anything.

Hard to believe, considering how much I have to say these days, but true.

Poor social skills happen for two reasons: being insecure; and not learning adequate social skills in your childhood. Since I experienced both, I was definitely not speaking my mind. It's not only that I was scared to but I also literally didn't know how.

So how did I get from being a silent butterfly on the wall to being the Dr. Michelle Rozen you know today? You know, the confident one, the one who speaks on stages and TV? The one who makes 2 Second Decisions that changed her life and are about to change yours too? It didn't happen overnight, but this is what did it for me:

Winning decisions + hard work = wins = more confidence = speaking up and gaining much more impact

You can do it too, one winning decision at a time. You'll work hard. You'll gain wins. And then you'll look at yourself and ask: who is this confident person who speaks up and has gained so much impact?

I'll tell you who that person is.

YOU.

~~DIDN'T SPEAK~~

~~DIDN'T TAKE A STAND~~

~~DIDN'T SAY WHAT I THINK~~

SPOKE MY MIND

CHAPTER SIXTEEN

MOTIVATE YOURSELF AND OTHERS

"Once you know what failure feels like, determination chases success." –Kobe Bryant

I am going to divide this chapter into two. In the first part I want to talk to you about motivating yourself. I want to talk about how motivation works in the human mind, and how you can get yourself motivated and keep yourself motivated. You will hear some people say that motivation doesn't matter. That is not true. Discipline matters. Structure matters. Mind hacks to get things done matter. But without the flame of motivation, your fire will be very, very small. Motivation is what fuels passion. I want to talk to you about the passion of motivation, where it comes from, and how you keep that fire burning.

In the second part of this chapter I want to talk about motivating others. In order to succeed, you really need other people. As a leader, you need to motivate your team. As a parent, you need to know how to motivate your kids to do what you want them to do.

One of my psychology professors back when I was in my PhD program was probably one of the worst professors I ever had. Sometimes he would not show up to classes, and sometimes he would show up unprepared and talk about things not related to anything even remotely close to what we were dealing with. He was messy. He was all over the place. Literally the worst. But I came to learn in life that **wisdom comes from**

the most unpredictable people. I had so many wonderful professors and I can't remember most of what they talked about. But this one forgot once again one day that he had class, then all of a sudden showed up 20 minutes late, and with only a few students remaining started talking to us about this and that as if nothing happened. I don't even remember what the conversation was about, but I vividly remember him suddenly throwing his head backwards, laughing, and saying, "Well, nobody ever changed their behavior just because they were told to, right?"

Freeze.

Think.

Nobody ever changed their behavior just because they were told to.

Nobody ever becomes motivated just because they are told to.

Nobody ever tries harder just because they are told to.

Come on.

How many times have you had these conversations with your kids? Words and words and more words about what they need to fix and work harder on.

How many times have you had these conversations with people at work? Explaining to team members what they need to do, why they need to work as a team, and why this is so important.

Nobody ever changed their behavior just because they were told to.

So if words don't work, and lectures don't work, and talks don't work, what does? What motivates people around you, at home and work, to do what you want them to do?

We will talk about that in the second half of this chapter.

But for now let's start with you.

The three pillars of motivation

THERE ARE THREE pillars of motivation, both of yourself and of others. I call them the 3 Ps of Motivation:

The Three Pillars (3 Ps) of Motivation

Perception

Proficiency

Purpose

As we talk about motivating yourself and then shifting from there to motivating others, you will realize that the 3 Ps of motivation apply to both yourself and others, only in different ways. Let's start with your motivation of yourself.

Pillar # 1: Perception

Perception is all about how you see yourself in the context of your life. Many people talk about mindset in the context of motivation, but mindset actually results from perception. If you perceive yourself as someone who is capable, you will become more motivated because you believe you can, and believe you deserve to be successful. Your mindset is the result of your self-perception. By contrast, if you believe you are not as good as others and that success is hard to reach, you will become less motivated, because you will perceive yourself as someone who is not capable. Success will seem out of reach within your perception of yourself and your chances to succeed.

You will hear people say that it is all in your head. Well, it sure is. If you believe in yourself, you will be motivated and driven. If you believe you stand no chance, why would you be motivated?

And so the question is not "how do I motivate myself?" The question is "how do I believe in myself?"

The way you perceive yourself is the key to your mindset and motivation. If you perceive yourself as someone who can, you become more motivated. No one is motivated to do something if they don't think they can succeed.

The other aspect of motivation is that you perceive the goal as something you actually care about. It has to matter to you at a 10. Otherwise you simply don't care.

This is what a 2 Second Decision sounds like for something that you care about greatly:

How much do I want this job? 0 to 10? 100.

How much do I want to save my marriage? 0 to 10? 100,000.

Get the picture?

If you perceive the goal as something you care about (10 and above, which means you really care), and you perceive yourself as someone who can go for it if they set their mind for it, you have given yourself the great fire of motivation.

> Motivation = I really want this + I perceive myself as someone who can get it if I try really hard

If you think about it that way, the problem then becomes why we are not motivated. The issue is that we may be focusing on things that don't actually matter to us the most. If your family matters to you, and you perceive yourself as a responsible parent and spouse, you will figure out ways to discipline yourself to keep your job, pay your bills, and stay healthy for your family. If stabilizing yourself financially really matters to you, and you perceive yourself as a hard-working, capable person, you will get a second job and discipline yourself to budget better. First you have to want to, and perceive yourself as capable. Then comes the role of discipline. Discipline is critical to success, but without the fire of motivation you will not have the enthusiasm that causes people to exceed their limits. They have to first want to really badly, and believe that they can; then comes the hard work and discipline, and then success.

> "Believe you can and you're halfway there."
> –Theodore Roosevelt

Pillar #2: Proficiency

Proficiency is the most important skill there is. No one taught you that skill at school, but without it you will have a hard time keeping yourself motivated and succeeding. What I am referring to is the skill of setting and achieving goals. Proficiency in goal setting is something fundamental you need to have, like reading or writing. Once you know how to do it, you will manage your life completely differently, and you will never look back again.

Some people would say, "I already have goals. I don't need to set any." You will find a lot of time what these people actually have are wishes and aspirations. Not only do they not have any set goals, they also don't know how to set them, because they have never actually done it. They do not have proficiency in setting goals, a proficiency you must have.

People who say this also often say that their "goals" are to be rich, thin, happy, successful, and live their dreams. But these are not goals; they are wishes common to all humans.

When you have proficiency in setting goals, you have the confidence and motivation to know what you are doing, and to know you are going to succeed in doing it.

Here's the great news: this proficiency in setting goals is not complicated. it is not rocket science and anyone can do it. Here is how it works:

A goal is a result of focused effort in the direction of something very important to you. It:

1. Is well-defined (lose 50 pounds, save $10,000, finish my degree)
2. Requires work
3. Must have a deadline

Setting goals helps in triggering new behaviors, guiding your focus, and sustaining momentum in life. Goals also help align your focus and promote a sense of self-mastery. In the end, you can't manage what you don't measure, and you can't improve upon something that you don't properly manage.

You may say, "I don't know how to set goals. I can try but I've never actually done it that way before." No wonder. You can get a Master's degree at a leading university and never receive a single hour of instruction on goal setting and achieving.

Fortunately goal setting is a skill, like time management, swimming or skiing. And all skills are *learnable*. Once you learn how to do it, and repeat it over and over again, it will become an ingrained part of you and how you do things.

And here is the best part of it all: from the very first day you begin setting goals, the progress you will make and the successes you will enjoy will astonish you.

Can anything be more motivating that that?

Pillar #3: Purpose

According to the Merriam-Webster Dictionary, purpose is the feeling of being determined to do or achieve something. There are many books that have impacted my life and thinking, but if you ask me which of them has had the greatest impact on me and still does, I would say it is Victor Frankl's *Man's Search for Meaning*. Written during the Holocaust, basically all modern research on purpose has their origins in this single book. While Frankl was a prisoner at several Nazi concentration camps, he noticed that his fellow prisoners who had a sense of purpose showed greater resilience to the torture, labor and starvation they had to endure. He found a partial explanation for this in a quote from Friedrich Nietzsche: "Those who have a 'why' to live, can bear almost any 'how.'" In his book he talks about the crucial role of meaning and purpose.

Several studies show that purpose protects people in situations of difficult circumstances. Now here is the most interesting part. Frankl has argued, based in part of his own observations in the concentration camps, and in part on his research, that **adversity actually contributes to the development of purpose in life**. In other words, if you use adversity as your fuel, you will become more successful than you ever thought was possible. Your adversity may be your gift in disguise.

Purpose is the foundation of motivation, and you are the only source of it. No one can tell you to have purpose. It is deep within you. I often hear people say, "I don't know what my purpose is." I am here to tell you: use 2 Second Decisions and find out your 10s, because you will never be motivated on your 2s. Then find your fire and start living the life you actually want to live.

Your 10s do not have to be big. I will share my biggest 10 with you, and it may surprise you. My 10 is my family. Everything I have ever done, I have done for them. I love Adam and my kids. This family is my masterpiece. And for them I am willing to be so out of my comfort zone that I don't even remember when the last time was that I was in it. I am so focused around my family that I am willing to do anything, deal with anything, and challenge myself with anything.

Your 10s do not have to be about saving the world or doing something grand. Some days my 10 leads me to writing another article and going on TV. Another day my 10 causes me to do the laundry at 10 o'clock at night. But I know my 10 and it gives me joy, clarity and strength. Your 10 may be simple, it may be silly, it may even be something you don't want to share with others. People didn't survive the Holocaust because they wanted to bring world peace. They survived because they wanted to see someone they loved again. Life is not that complicated. We are all passionate about different things. Find your 10s.

How to motivate other people—your team, your clients, your kids, your spouse—to do what you want them to do

Now let's take the three Ps of motivation and look at how they work for motivating other people—team members, clients, kids, even your spouse—to work with you rather than against you toward your goals.

Motivating other people through perception

Perception in the context of motivating other people is all about getting out of your own head. If you check your interactions with other people around you, especially when you need something from them and they are not reacting in the way you expect them to, you will find that a lot of them revolve around blaming and accusing. This behavior is literally all about staying in your own head. You perceive yourself as just and right in what you are asking, and then you perceive the other person as difficult, not willing enough, or not caring enough.

Get out of your own head and learn to give other people the benefit of a doubt. Perceive them as good. Perceive them as willing. And then direct them to do what you want them to do. Did you ever consider that if someone is not motivated to do things for you, a lot of it has to do with you? With how you interact with them?

Because we are living in our own heads, it is so easy to perceive the other person as difficult and unwilling, because it puts the weight of the interaction on them and relieves you from accountability. Did you remember to recognize your team member for the great job they did? Did you get out of your own head to see how challenging it was for them, and how hard they have worked? Did you thank them? Did you remember to hug your kid for a job well done? To thank your spouse for something nice they did? Even if you think that they should have done more, all of them, we are not in the 'being right' business here, and we are not in the 'keeping score' business either. We are in the business of motivating other people to do what we want them to do, remember? So, setting aside the fact that you may be right, because it really doesn't matter, make sure to recognize them. Thank them. Lead with gratitude. Lead with compassion. And first and foremost, lead. Because when you blame or complain you do not lead. Choosing to lead is in your hands.

Motivate other people through proficiency

There is a know-how aspect to motivating others. Once you know how to do it, motivating others to work with you rather than against you towards your goals will become second nature to you. The know-how for motivating other people is actually quite simple: help them succeed, believe in them, and celebrate their success. Your role as a leader is to elevate others, to help them succeed. Look around you. Every person in your team, every person in your life, wants to feel good about themselves. What happens if you complain all the time, judge and criticize? They will work against you, even if they don't tell you that to your face. In their mind, they are not on the same team with you.

Years ago, I was on an overnight flight with my husband, flying back from Vegas to New York. I was tired and all I wanted to do was get home. I was dreaming of a good shower and getting some sleep. At the end of the flight, I noticed that all the passengers were sitting with their phones directed to the front of the plane. I turned my tired head to Adam and asked, "What's going on?"

Adam replied, "Bill Clinton is on the flight."

Personally, I didn't think much of it. First of all, I don't really care for famous people; and second of all, I was mostly thinking about how quickly I can get to that hot shower and catch up on some sleep. Adam, on the other hand, had completely different plans. He of course had to be the only guy who chased Bill Clinton out of the plane, waiving his hand up in the air and calling, "Mr. Clinton! Mr. Clinton!"

Well, sure enough, Clinton stopped, turned around toward Adam, and started this whole three- or four-minute conversation with him right there at the airport, not knowing him and really having no reason at all to do so, with his hand on Adam's shoulder the whole time. He was completely present and into the conversation, and then parted ways with Adam as if they were old friends. I stood there completely fascinated by the whole thing and absolutely amazed.

Clinton had no reason to give Adam his undivided attention. But he did. Because this is how he does things. Now, politics aside, this was an amazing lesson in how you motivate other people. It is simple and human but we all forget how to do it.

You motivate other people by showing them they matter to you.

You give them your undivided attention.

You recognize them.

You see them.

People want to matter.

Did you know that every time you give someone a genuine compliment, it triggers the same area in their brain as receiving cash? Now I want you to stop and think: how many people did you actually give a genuine compliment to in the past week?

Let me guess. Not enough.

Motivate other people through purpose

Purpose as a source of motivation is critical. When we spoke about your motivation on an individual level, we spoke about purpose as an incredibly powerful force. We also said that a strong sense of purpose creates very powerful resilience. The same comes into play when you motivate others. Expecting people to do things because 'you said so,' as the leader or parent, doesn't go very far. It is the purpose, the 'why,' behind it that makes it sustainable.

As a leader, purpose is what drives the team. You must stop and define to yourself first: why does your team do what it does? Why does it matter? Where are you making a difference for your customers, and where doesn't the individual responsibilities of each team member come into play within the context of that purpose?

Get clear with yourself and get clear with your team: what is the unique contribution of each team member? You should be able to define each team member's unique contribution, including your own. Together, all of these unique contributions should align with your overall mission and create the winning force that you all become together. I want you to practice the same within your family as well (families are teams just as much). What is the unique contribution of each of you? Together, it makes you the unique and strong force that you are. Unique contributions aligned around one purpose is the true power of what a winning team is all about.

~~I SHOULD HAVE~~

~~I WOULD HAVE~~

~~I COULD HAVE~~

I DID

You Got This: Get in the Driver's Seat of Your Life, Work and Courage

Dear Success Warrior,

I want to see you steering the wheel and in the driver's seat of your life.

You may think that life has thrown you in different directions, and that may very well be the case. But no matter where you are, how bad you got knocked down on your knees, until the last day of your life on this earth you have control.

You have control, you have choices, and you are in charge.

And the more you claim that control and take charge of your life, work and future, the more successful and happy you are going to be.

The more you get in the driver's seat of your life, the less fear you are going to experience.

Fear takes over when you feel like you don't have control. You beat fear when you take control, when you get in the driver's seat.

You can manage your time differently. You can handle your relationships, at home and work, differently. You can make 2 Second Decisions at any point of your day that will give you control over yourself, your day, and ultimately your life.

Scaling things for yourself—what is right for you and what is not right for you—within 2 seconds is not rocket science. Anyone can do it. All you need to do is to get out of your own head and give it a number.

How right is a certain choice for you? How much do you want it?

Is it 1?
Is it 2?
Is it 3?
Is it 4?
Is it 5?
Is it 6?
Is it 7?
Is it 8?
Is it 9?
Is it 10?

Get out of your own head. Give it a number. And then take action.

Your life, work and courage will change in the most amazing and wonderful ways. You got this.

GET IN THE DRIVER'S SEAT OF YOUR LIFE, WORK AND COURAGE.

YOUR FUTURE IS IN YOUR HANDS.

Made in the USA
Monee, IL
23 March 2021